1

YOURSELF
PUBLICITY

FOR THOSE TOO CHEAP
OR TOO BROKE
TO HIRE A PUBLICIST

PHYLLIS CADDELL-M

First Edition

Do-It-Yourself Publicity: For Those Too Cheap or Too Broke to Hire A Publicist
Phyllis Caddell-M
Edited By: Lithobit Publishing

ISBN 0-9770745-1-x

Cover Design by Two2TangoDesign, two2tangoworks@earthlink.net
Production Design by Tamburello Productions, r12n@earthlink.net

For speaking engagements, consulting, publicity workshops,
or to subscribe to the Do-It-Yourself newsletter

Please log onto www.phylliscaddell.com

**Do-It-Yourself Publicity: For Those Too Cheap
Or Too Broke To Hire A Publicist**
Published by Lithobit Publishing
120 N. Orange Grove Blvd., Pasadena, CA 91103 USA

Copyright 2006
Phyllis Caddell-M

CONTENTS

Preface—Note to the Reader

<u>Do-It-Yourself Publicity: For Those Too Cheap Or Too Broke To Hire A Publicist</u> is a book designed to provide the fundamentals of public relations in order to effectively launch a publicity campaign.

This book is for any driven person with an entrepreneurial spirit who may not be in a financial position or simply doesn't want to spend the money to hire a professional publicist, but need the proper tools and knowledge to successfully launch a publicity campaign.

After reading this book you will be aware of the necessary information and on your way to understanding and creating a press release, biography, fact sheet, pitch letter, and a media alert. You will also be able to assemble a press kit, understand and identify the media, and function as a "DIY" (Do-It-Yourself) publicist.

You will read short stories of the author's experience as a publicist, and sharpen your skills with the pop quiz and case problems provided.

Although this is not the only public relations book on the market, it will educate, enlighten and entertain you giving you the courage and excitement to get out there and do it yourself!

Acknowledgments

I dedicate this book to my Lord and savior Jesus Christ for without you I am nothing. To my wonderful loving husband Zenon Christopher M who supports and loves me unconditionally. And to my family Doris "Ya Ya," Caddell, Osker "Papa" Caddell, Dayna Caddell, Brenda Caddell, Traci Caddell Williams, Nicholas Vann Clayton, Brandon Caddell, Fred Williams, and Doretha Riley. I love you all.

To my friends and associates, you know who you are and how much you've supported me. Thank you.

Thank you Professor Don Silvis for being an excellent college instructor.

Thank you Asha Tyson, Alvin Williams and Jefflyn Dangerfield for your guidance and encouraging words that helped me complete this book.

To all the artists and clients I've worked with—Rock On!

Warning-Disclaimer

This book is designed to provide information creating and implementing your own publicity campaign for yourself, business or product. It is sold with the understanding that the publisher and author are not engaged in rendering legal or other professional services. If legal or other expert assistance is required, the services of a competent professional should be sought.

You are urged to read all the available material, learn as much as you can about publicity, and tailor the information to your needs.

Anyone who decides to launch a publicity campaign or practice public relations must expect to invest a lot of time and effort into it.

Every effort has been made to make this book as complete and as accurate as possible. However there *may be mistakes,* both typographical and in content. Therefore, this book should be used only as a general guide and not as the ultimate source of public relations and publicity information.

The purpose of this book is to complement, amplify and supplement other texts. The author and *Lithobit Publishing* shall have neither liability nor responsibility to any person or entity with respect to any loss or damage caused, or alleged to have been caused, directly or indirectly, by the information contained in this book.

DO-IT-YOURSELF PUBLICITY

FOR THOSE TOO CHEAP OR TOO BROKE TO HIRE A PUBLICIST

PHYLLIS CADDELL-M

1
GETTING NOTICED

Picture this. You're standing in the middle of a mall and you start to sing obnoxiously loud for at least fifteen minutes. You cause a scene and are led away by mall security. You are definitely noticed but what is your purpose? Are you trying to promote your new CD? Get a record deal? Or go to jail?

Publicity is the art of getting noticed. Getting noticed, by the right audience or public at the right time. It is a process that requires specific planning, detailing, and excellent follow-up skills.

A more subtle and professional approach to getting noticed is to open your mouth and let people know who you are, what you have to offer, and especially how they will benefit. I've always found networking to be key in spreading the word. Conferences, seminars and mixers are the best platforms, but you must come prepared. Always have a business card and a thirty-second pitch to sell yourself to anyone who may ask, "So what do you do?" If you are prepared in advance you're guaranteed to make a lasting impression.

Be sure to keep your friends and family abreast of your goals. If you're looking for exposure let it be known. If you're having an art show or performance make sure they spread the word. You can always count on people talking. Eventually someone you may have told, about your product or service, will tell the right person and voila! You're on your way. You get a phone call from someone inquiring about your services. Don't be afraid. This is it! This is the opportunity to use your thirty-second sell. Sell yourself to the caller. Make them comfortable, get them to open up and most of all get them to say yes, at least to a meeting.

Positioning, selling yourself or getting noticed is a full-time commitment that brings major results if done correctly. The drawbacks? There are none unless you don't try. The benefits are plenty. But if you don't tell the world what you have to offer, at least your friends and family to start, no one else will.

Remember the saying "nothing from nothing leaves nothing?" Well, take heed because while you're sitting at home wondering how you will launch your publicity campaign, there are thousands of assertive people pushing you further down the ladder of success.

This book is an ingredient to becoming a successful "DIY" publicist. Now get going and make me proud!

2

PUBLICIST, PUBLIC RELATIONS, PUBLICITY, ADVERTISING, MARKETING
Will Somebody Please Make It Clear?

In my seventeen years of practicing PR people have addressed me as a publisher, a marketing consultant, an advertising consultant, a promotions expert, and just about any other title in the communications field. I used to get so frustrated and tired of correcting each person who called my office wanting to know more about our publishing services or advertising rates. I could not believe how little people knew of the field I studied so hard to earn a college degree.

I will admit that because public relations is a component of most marketing initiatives and often work together with promotions and advertising campaigns, the terms can easily be misunderstood by the unfamiliar. So before we get started it would be a crime if I did not explain the differences.

Publicist

Publicists are specialists who practice public relations who prepare and distribute publicity material through various mediums using various tools (press releases, brochures, media alerts, etc.). Although the same principles apply in all areas of public relations, publicists work in diverse fields and have different publics. One publicist may work at a hospital and coordinate black-tie events to raise money for the cancer wing. Another may write speeches for the president, while another may obtain appropriate publicity or media coverage for music tours.

Aside from keeping a good working-relationship with the media, the publicist's day is mostly spent on writing press releases, creating press kits (electronic and hard copy), pitching the media and researching various outlets for numerous opportunities. They put in long hours and they operate under hectic conditions. They must stick to strict deadlines especially when they overlap with publicity events, such as the release of a book or an award show. They have to make sure that they send appropriate and accurate information to mediums in time for an event they are generating publicity for, such as a record release or grand opening. And they must, by all means, know how to chew gum and walk at the same time.

Public Relations

People often refer to public relations without knowing exactly what it means. It is an essential part of today's world with so many dynamics that the full reality of what public relations is, is impossible to fully understand to the novice consumer.

Although the terms publicity and public relations are often mistakenly used interchangeably, public relations is the umbrella term that publicity falls under. It involves research and analysis, and feedback from the public.

Public Relations is the art of analyzing trends, predicting their consequences, and implementing planned programs of action. It is used to inform, persuade, create and make things happen by using a number of communication tools including, but not limited to, brochures, fact sheets, newsletters, press releases, workshops and seminars.

Public Relations is the art of creating a favorable atmosphere for marketing a product or service. When a client wins a Grammy or an Emmy award you will find favorable stories and headlines in many newspapers and magazines applauding their accomplishments. You will also see them on evening and morning TV talk shows. But when disaster strikes, say your client, who happens to be a celebrity, is found guilty for drug trafficking or spousal abuse, it is the publicists job to act as the client's spokesperson evaluating the circumstances and the damages quickly by assembling all facts and giving the media information in the clients favor. Public relations is always a gamble, but when implemented correctly it creates instant credibility, which is something advertising can never accomplish.

Publicity

Publicity is under the public relations umbrella. It is the disbursement of information about an event, individual, project or company. Publicity appears in newspapers, magazines and on television shows, and creates awareness, builds images and influences opinions and decisions.

The impact of publicity is priceless. It provides credibility that opens doors, establishes one as an expert in their field, and it sells a service or product.

A way to establish instant credibility, for yourself, is to write an article or two for a publication or have someone write an article that quotes you as an expert in your field. Your name in print, especially if you're quoted in an article, makes a believer out of most who read it. If you send a press release about your new invention and it is printed by hundreds of newspapers that is instant publicity which will lead to the selling of your product. The same goes for a service introduced to the public through various media outlets. Once the word gets out hold on because it will definitely be a fast ride.

Advertising

Advertising is the paid promotion of goods, services, companies and ideas by an identified sponsor. Marketers see advertising as part of an overall promotional strategy. The most common or general way to describe advertising is space and time in print, electronic media (TV, radio) and other mediums as bus stop benches, buses and billboards. Companies or individuals contract to purchase space (print) and time (electronic), and their ad is printed or broadcast exactly as they prepared it. A feature article in a newspaper or magazine, or an appearance on a TV talk show provides instant credibility and goes farther than an ad giving the reader a chance to see you as a person as well as your business and the service you provide. An ad is simply created, purchased and placed. Anyone with a budget can place an ad whether it's true or not.

If you want exposure and are not big on taking chances, buy an ad. If you're an optimist and would like to position yourself as a credible professional, try your hand at publicity.

Marketing

Although marketing is about the advertising and/or personal selling of goods and services, there's much more to it.

Marketing entails identifying the particular wants and needs of a target market of customers, and satisfying those customers better than the competitors. This involves doing market research on customers, analyzing their needs, and then making strategic decisions about:

- Product design - the product management aspect of marketing deals with the specifications of the actual good or service, and how it relates to the end-user's needs and wants.
- Pricing - the process of setting a price for a product, including discounts.
- Promotion - advertising, sales-promotion, publicity, and personal selling, and refers to the various methods of promoting the product, brand, or company.
- Distribution - refers to how the product gets to the customer; for example, point of sale placement or retailing

3

THE POWER OF PUBLICITY

Today nothing is exclusive. We live in a cookie-cutter world and it's getting less creative everyday. Think about it. How many black BMW's and Range Rovers can you count on the street in one day? How many times has the same music track been recycled for a different recording artist? Why are so many entertainers morphing into each other and so many young girls trying desperately to look like Beyoncé or Britney Spears? Where is the originality? The freshness? It's very limited and that is one reason why a good publicity campaign, implemented effectively and creatively, can make a world of difference. Or at least get you noticed.

The effective publicity campaign can convince an audience that bikinis are popular to wear in Wisconsin. In December! It's about positioning, timing and convincing, and with proper publicity many opportunities become available.

The power of publicity is amazing if you know how to use it to your advantage. Recognition or publicity is vital in every area of business including law, medicine, art, beauty, fashion and technology. Because there are so many professionals seeking exposure (radio airtime, TV and publication placements) mediums are bombarded for the same slots. Before getting in the game, your service, product or company should represent you in the most professional, creative way possible.

Exposure in the print and electronic mediums, for example, can favorably position you, your product or service tremendously. It will also boost the volume of business, or provide information that may sway the consumer to patronize your service or business rather than your competitor.

The average consumer who is exposed to a business or service through foot traffic is likely to try the service once or twice. But the consumer who reads a published article, about a business or service, in the local or national paper is more likely to choose this hands down. Why? The average consumer is conditioned to believe that what they read in a feature of a notable publication, or what they see on television is the truth. If it's in the media it's instant validation.

If you read about a doctor who specializes in hair transplants and the article lists testimonies of former clients with before and after photos, you would probably be more apt to patronize this company more so than the hair transplant salon you saw in an ad with before and after photos. How do you know the ad is real? The doctor could have had any graphic artist manipulate the before-and-after photos.

The same goes for TV. Would you buy a thirty-minute teeth whitening product advertised on a commercial or infomercial, or would you buy the same type of product after Oprah try the product on live TV, and her teeth turn whiter within the one-hour show?

Now do you understand what I mean? When it comes to publicity the type of placement is very important.

4
WRITING, WRITING AND MORE WRITING
An essential skill to PR survival

For those of you who think public relations is all about throwing a party, talking or schmoozing, think again. Eighty percent of a publicist job is writing. Whether it's a pitch letter or a press release, if it's news, before the media receives it, it has to be written. Unless you are planning to hire a freelance writer or press release writing service it is essential that you learn the fundamentals of PR writing.

PITCH LETTER

The pitch letter is the first document the media will see when opening your press kit. That is enough to let you know how important it is to put your best foot forward when writing the pitch.

The pitch letter is simply a letter to the media selling your product, company, service or event. It is straight to the point giving pertinent information, and is exciting or interesting enough that the editor will want to view the material in your press kit. It is never too long or boring where it ends up in the trash can nor is it too sweet where the editor can read between the lines and see that you're trying too hard. But most of all it should never try to sway or form an opinion for the reader. That's an instant turn off.

The first paragraph tells the reader why you're writing, what you want and how the subject appeals to their audience. The second and third paragraphs support the first paragraph with newsworthy facts about your product, company, service or event listed by bullet points or sentences. I prefer the latter because it's easier to read and it stands out.

In closing, tell the reader that you will follow up with them in a few days to discuss your request. Try to avoid telling the reader to contact you if they are interested. Even though the media is always looking for news, you are asking for a favor in your letter so it would behoove you to follow up with a phone call or email to try to close the deal.

When you have completed the letter, if time permits, walk away from it and come back to it for a final read. This will give you time to make any changes or additions before sending it out with your package.

In addition, make sure salutations are accurate. Is the person married or single? Do they prefer you use their first name only, or full name including middle initial? If a therapist has a column and you send a letter to Mr. Jeffries but he clearly uses Dr. Jeffries, you've made a terrible mistake big enough to land your package in the trash or at least in the "less likely to read" pile. Also, never act as if you know someone if you don't. Addressing someone by their first name is an iffy situation unless this is what they prefer.

BIOGRAPHY

Whether you start with a quote, question, or fact a biography to promote a company, CEO, producer, or recording artist is mandatory because it gives the recipient needed background information. It should be no more than two pages and filled with relevant information. If its three pages you better make sure it's very interesting and pertinent. The bio should list accolades, contacts and any other information relevant to the press kit. Listing a person's favorite food or color is fluff and doesn't matter unless it is relevant to the pitch.

The main function of the bio is to provide the recipient with enough background information that after reading they can asses an intelligent and knowledgeable over view. More importantly the recipient will be able to intelligently recite or forward accurate information about the subject if necessary.

There are three parts to a biography:

1. **The beginning** of the bio usually starts with who the person is, or the launch or inception of a product or company.

2. **The body** will support the beginning with details and is usually filled with information like accolades, collaborations, and how a project came together or how a relationship was formed.

3. **The end** will usually list collaborations, organization memberships, family information, and hobbies.

The biography should be updated as often as information changes in your life, career, or company.

If you have no other component, for your press kit, it should contain a bio. Make sure it is professional, detailed and reads with ease. More importantly, if you are not a writer don't write. Hire a professional, friend or colleague who is well written.

MEDIA ALERT

A media alert is a short one-page document that resembles an invitation. It highlights the important information without the fluff of a press release focusing on the five W's of journalism – who, what, when, where, why, and sometimes how.

The media alert is sent to the media as a reminder of what was sent in the initial press release regarding an event. It is wise to send it to the media, via fax or email, the day before or the morning of, to ensure coverage. Because the media are sent so much information on a daily basis, they constantly need reminders.

There have been times when a TV crew was scheduled to cover an event but it was canceled due to bad weather so they chose the next best event that was being held at an inside venue. Because a media alert landed on the news assignment desk, the same day of the event, the media had a story and the sender was successful in securing coverage.

THE FACT SHEET

Although fact sheets are distributed to the same media as a press release and media alert, they are in outline form instead of in news story format.

A fact sheet is essentially a quick reference tool for the media: it summarizes the key points about an event, product, or a company to help reporters get a quick grasp or overview.   It's a media cheat sheet if you will.

When a talk show-host is familiarizing themselves with guests they read the fact sheet because it is organized with bullet points, and it highlights the most important facts about the guest.

THE PRESS RELEASE

Of all the tools publicists use, the press release is the most common. It is the primary written method of conveying news to the media for publication or broadcast placement. It sells a product or a service, a person or an event and is as good as it is conveyed.

Because the press release is often the first or second item the producer, talent booker, editor or reporter looks for in a press kit it requires careful preparation. It also requires well thought-out distribution so that it is delivered to the right place in an accurate, timely, easily usable manner.

Like the biography, the press release can start with a question, fact or quote, and is a simple document with information in ready-to-publish form. The typical release is one-to-two pages and includes information about a company, service, product or event. The editors of print and broadcast media, to whom releases are sent, judge them on the basis of news interest for their audience and timeliness. Releases should be prepared so that the media can easily relay the information to their audience with ease.

The next time you watch TV check out *Access Hollywood* or *Extra* and notice how the news is reported. It's actually a verbal press release.

A press release faces intense competition when it arrives on an editor's desk. As they scan, and I do mean scan the release, editors make almost instant decisions, assigning each release to one of three categories:

News. Information that is certain to be used.

Maybe. Stories possibly worth developing if a reporter has the time.

Discard. A press release of insufficient interest to the receiving editor's audience and those of insignificant value that would require too much energy to develop. These go into the wastebasket!

Media personnel often receive hundreds of press releases a day. They know immediately if they are interested in a story. If not, they toss it in the trash.

They also can detect truth from hype. So, as my college professor would say, "stay away from the fluff and stick to the facts."

Press releases that are prepared properly have the best chance of being accepted for publication, assuming that their content is newsworthy.

Tips To Ensure Your Press Release Make The News Or Get Noticed.

- Make sure the information is newsworthy.
- Ask yourself, "How are people going to relate to this and will they be able to connect?"
- Make sure the first 10 words of your release are effective, as they are the most important.
- Avoid excessive use of adjectives and fancy language.
- Deal with the facts.
- Provide as much contact information as possible: contact person, address, phone, fax, email, and web site address.
- Make sure you wait until you have something with enough substance to issue a release.
- Make it as easy as possible for media representatives to do their jobs.

Any New Angle Can Create News

Once a press release, on a specific topic, has been written and distributed, that is just the beginning. The fun is about to start. Your link between your company or product, and the media is just being established. The key to establishing this "bond" or link is to send out multiple press releases by creating news flashes with every new angle. A new angle gives you an excuse to send an update in a short release.

For example, record companies send out releases every time a new recording project is being released. Whether it is an executive gain or loss, or a new artist or artist promo tour, each warrants a press release.

A very good example of this is when my company was hired to work the new Shirley Caesar project. There were a plethora of reasons we needed to distribute press releases.

1. This was her 41st project and a lot was happening in her life. 2. She was releasing her project on her own label for the first time. 3. She performed with Alicia Keys at a benefit concert. 4. Her project debut at number 3 on the Billboard charts. Need I go on?

At the same time you don't have to have a huge happening to send out a release to remind the media of your existence. On a smaller scale, Delord Skincare added a new skincare package to their existing line. The press release was entitled, "Delord Skincare Introduces The All-In-One Skincare Solution," and was sent to beauty trades.

No matter what is going on with your client or company, always look for a reason or angle to send out a press release as long as it is newsworthy. But remember don't overdo it to where the media is immune to your releases and begin to ignore you. The key is to release just enough so your client looks busy.

Something To Think About

1. A good press release cuts to the chase and digs out the meat. The media want facts, short and to the point. Less is more.

2. When updating your press release ask at least three colleagues or friends whom you trust to proofread your work. Everyone has different strengths and will more than likely help to improve the quality of your press release.

3. Be aware of what topics are discussed in publications and what type of ads they carry. These factors will tell you if your press release is newsworthy to that particular outlet.

4. Look for indications as to what is newsworthy to the media outlet you are considering. Are entertainment stories featured? Is there a beauty or fashion section? What types of feature stories are placed? Then figure out how your release fits their format.

5. Don't send out press releases blindly. Study every publication before sending your carefully constructed press release. If you want to cover the Internet, check out as many outlets in the category you wish to target in much the same way. Do your homework like the media does theirs.

How To Get The Best Press Release Headline

When I was in college one of my professors, who I'll never forget, told my news writing class, "if you want an attention-grabbing headline for a press release read the *Los Angeles Times* metro section and the front page of any major newspaper." That piece of information has been very true and helpful. Why is this so important? The average person doesn't like to search for anything; car keys, a parking space, a phone number, let alone a story imbedded in a page of long-winded words. If you're pressed for time, which most of us are, and you want to read the newspaper, you might scan the article titles and subheadings because they tell a lot about a story. More than likely if we like what we see in the heading, chances are we'll read the entire article.

Headings entice and inform the reader. The next time you entitle your press release, think of how it would appear as a newspaper headline.

Note: Write the heading first if you want to use it as a guide to the content of your release; write it after you write the release if you want it to summarize the contents.

Why Write a Press Release and How Often Do You Send One?

A press release is perhaps the most efficient, most economical way of advertising your product, business or service to a broad audience. Because the media need news to fill their empty slots they pick up press releases easily and frequently. The media also need to inform and entertain their audiences therefore, the more unique and interesting your press release presentation is, the more likely it is to appeal to media and chances of getting your information published will be increased dramatically.

In today's fast paced world of communication sending just one press release to the media generally will not suffice. While you don't want to overdo it it's important to keep your news on the forefront of media attention. Therefore distributing press releases once a month is a good barometer to measure media interest. The trick is to keep the media informed with a twist. Try this. Send your initial release, summarizing the content of your press release message in the title. This will be used as your base. Each time you send an additional release, pertaining to the same subject, add new information at the beginning of the release and alter your title to match the new news. Brief reminders of who and what the person or product is about should be included in each consecutive release. When you run out of new interest, find a new angle of your product or service and start the process again. Remember that every update you make to your product or business is essentially news and each addition or change to your product or business is news. If it isn't newsworthy don't bother.

To get the readers attention you must reach out to their needs and interests, not yours. If they can relate to your message you've got them.

More Tips:

1. Grab the reader in the first 3 seconds or you lose them. Start with an

interesting fact for example: Is acutane killing teens? Studies show that several teens that use acutane for acne commit suicide.

2.   Use charts, bullets and boldface to outline pertinent facts within the body of the release.

3.   Start your release with an interesting quote. For example: Client of Celebrity hairstylist claims "My hair grew five inches in one month."

4.   Include information about your product or company on every release.

5.   Make the press release one page. No one wants to read on and on.

6.   Don't beat around the bush. Get to the point in the first paragraph.

DELIVERY OF THE PRESS RELEASE

The press release should be delivered to the media in a timely and effective manner. It should be addressed and sent to recipients, by name, to a selected target media source called micro-distribution or it may be sent in a broadside manner to large numbers of recipients, in an approach called macro-distribution. The best way to send a release is via email or fax. Most media outlets prefer email or fax but there are those who still prefer mail so do your research.

SUBMISSION OF THE PRESS RELEASE

Press releases are usually submitted to the news desk, unless they are clearly designed for a specific section or person. Although these specified sections operate separately, some liaison is maintained among them under the supervision of the managing editor to maintain balance and prevent duplication of effort. Don't think you're being thorough by sending a release to a specific editor, the managing editor, and news desk. You are clearly creating havoc.

A large newspaper like the *Los Angeles Times* or the *Chicago Tribune* receives hundreds of press releases every day, most of which end up in the trashcan. The majority of releases never have a chance of being published due to lack of relevance in the newspapers circulation area, arrive too late, or pertain to events so minor or so blatantly common that an editor throws it in the trash! Press releases must be relevant to the outlets it is being sent. You wouldn't send a food release to the fashion editor? Nor would you send the entertainment editor a beauty related release unless P. Diddy was releasing a skincare line. Remember a press release addressed to an editor by name has an advantage over one that is addressed to the managing editor or fashion editor.

ORGANIZATION OF A NEWSPAPER

Anyone practicing public relations should know how a newspaper is set up. Usually the publisher is the director of all financial, mechanical and administrative operations. The publisher also has an ultimate responsibility for news and editorial matters; in many instances they carry the title of editor or publisher depending on the size of the paper.

The editor heads the news and editorial department. The associate editor conducts the editorial and commentary pages and deals with the public concerning their content. The managing editor is the head of news operations to which the city editor, sports, business, entertainment, and lifestyle editors answer. The city editor directs the local news staff of reporters. Some members of the city staff cover community news as the police and city hall; others are on general assignment, meaning that they are sent to cover any type of story the city editor believes to be newsworthy.

APPEARANCE OF THE PRESS RELEASE

- Plain white 81/2-by 11-inch paper

- Specify release. Specify release in upper left hand corner. Immediate release if the information is for immediate publication. If a time restriction is necessary, as with an advance copy of a speech to be delivered at a specific hour, indicate the desired publication time; for example For Release at 4 p.m. EST June 14. This is called an embargo. Embargoes should be used only when genuinely necessary.

- Space. Leave 2 inches of space for editing convenience before starting the text.

- City and date. Always start the lead line with the city of where the company is based or where event is taking place and the date the release will be distributed to the press.

- Headline. Start the release with a headline. Not just any headline but an eye catching, attention-grabbing headline that will make the editor want to continue to read. After all, you are competing with other releases that come across the editor's desk. Type the headline in boldface; it can be one to three lines long.

- Lead. The news lead is the ideal "who, what, when, where, why, and how" opening of a straight news story. The advantage of using this type of lead is that even if the editor chops the rest of your story and leaves the first paragraph, your information is still printed with the most pertinent information.

- Feature Lead. This type of lead is written in a more entertaining way similar to the way magazine articles or television stories on Extra or Hollywood Access open. It's usually very clever or dramatic. The Metro section of the Los Angeles Times has great feature leads.

- Body. The body or text of the release comes after the lead. This is where you elaborate on the nature of the headline with background information, quotes from the CEO, designer, stylist, etc. and other relevant information vital to the story.

- If the release is more than one page always break the page by writing "more" at the bottom center of the page.

- The last section of the release can be a summary of the important points already touched on. If there is a contact for further information you can end with "for information, call or visit: telephone number, fax, email or Website. After two skipped lines end with # # # or –30- or END to let readers know they've reached the end of your release.

REASONS TO SEND A PRESS RELEASE

Use this list so you don't miss a chance to send a press release to newspapers, magazines, trade journals, radio and TV stations, online publications or newsletters.

Accomplishments

Alliance with another organization

Anniversary

Appearances on major events

Articles by or about you

Awards you are receiving

Books you have written

Community classes you are sponsoring

Company anniversary

Company name change

Company new address

Contest you are sponsoring

Contributions to charities, donations, scholarships

Death of major figure in your organization

Expanded facilities

Expanded hours

Ezine you are starting

Free classes

Free demonstrations

Free offer

Free samples

Fund-raising kick-off

Holiday events or programs

Hostile takeover

Incorporations

Industry awards or commendations

Industry programs in which you are participating

Job change

Land purchase

Mergers and acquisitions

Move into new market

New contract

New employees

New contracts, clients, customers

New products or services

Newsletter you are starting

Official announcement

Open house

Partnerships or strategic business alliances

Product recall

Public service announcements on radio/TV

Radio Show appearance

Rallies

Real estate transaction

Relocations

Research you are conducting, or results

Retirement

Sales promotions

Services for handicapped

Speaking engagement

Special events

Sponsorships

Strike

Tie-in with upcoming holidays

Tours of your company

Trade show where you are exhibiting

TV Show appearance

Website or new service online

Workshop or seminar you are presenting

Visit by celebrity or public figure

PRESS RELEASE DONT'S

The press release is often your only chance to make a great first impression. Publicists send hundreds of them each year. But so do many other people. That means confusing, inaccurate, pointless releases are the first to hit the newsroom trashcan.

To make sure yours isn't one of them, remember the following DONT'S at all times:

- Providing insufficient or inaccurate information. Particularly telephone numbers. Releases must be complete, accurate and specific.

- Writing too long. They should be no longer than two pages.

- Sending it too late. Mail, email or fax it at least three weeks before an event.

- Sending a release with no news value. News is what happens that is different. If it isn't different, it isn't news. Ask yourself this question before sending a release "Would anyone care besides me?" If the answer is yes, send the release. If no, do not send. Do not pass go!

- Omitting a contact name and phone number. At the top of the first page in the right hand corner, let editors know who they can call if they have questions.

- Calling after you send a release. Questions like "Did you get my news release?" or, "Do you know when, or if, it will be printed?" will brand you as a pest. This is very tricky and unless you have a relationship with whom you sent the release to you're going to have to hope and pray that what you sent was newsworthy enough to be used.

- Using outdated media reference books. Make sure the person to whom you are sending the press release still works there, and that the address is accurate. A press release sent to an editor who left the paper five years ago eventually will be routed to the right person, but they'll think you know nothing about the paper or who works there.

- Never send a blind release. Get the name of the person whom you're sending at all times when possible. If they refuse to give the name, in some cases they do, send the release to the assignment desk or news desk and cross your fingers that your release will be printed.

5

THE PRESS KIT
Packaging Yourself Creatively

After you or someone experienced have written the press release, bio, fact sheet, and pitch letter and picked publicity photos and other graphics, it's time to put it all together in a press kit.

When I first opened my PR firm I received a package I thought to be a press kit but after opening the envelope I was very surprised to see the disarray. There was no structure or organization to the kit. More importantly, there was no cover letter stating what the sender wanted me to do with the unsolicited information. So guess what happened to the package? That's right. I used it to practice my free throw shots. Bingo! In the trash it went with no regrets.

A press kit is a representation of you. If you were to attend a business meeting you wouldn't have only half the information for your presentation. So why would you prepare an incomplete press kit and send it out as if it were complete?

Often prepared when a company announces a new product, project, or event; a press kit gives the media a thorough background and provides information in various formats.

The basic press kit is a presentation folder with inside pockets. The left pocket houses press releases, fact sheets, bios, and the like. The right side holds photos, color slides, CD's and article clippings. Although this is how it is taught in school, today publicists are very creative in formatting press kits to their liking. The folder should be visually attractive, incorporating graphics when possible and overall appealing across the board.

If your package is "unsolicited"-meaning the recipient did not request it–it is close to impossible to get noticed. However, even solicited material must be in line with the guidelines to make a good first impression.

While teaching a public relations workshop an attendee asked, "How do I get attention when sending my press kit?" My answer was simply, "Do something to make your kit stand out from the rest." It's about being as creative as possible because let's face it society is hooked on looks and beats. We prefer pictures instead of words, the Internet instead of the encyclopedia, and we definitely would rather watch a video presentation with background music than a "blue suit" with a power point presentation.

Now that you know what it takes to grab the attention of the recipient, what do you include in the press kit to keep their interest and comply with the guidelines?

Product

Make sure the product in the kit is the best representation. If it's a CD with your music make sure the packaging is professional and of quality, and the first 30 to 60 seconds of the first track intrigues the recipient. If it's jewelry choose the best two to four pieces from your collection. The same goes for clothing designers, artists, etc.

EPK (Electronic Press kit)

The electronic press kit is a video or DVD presentation about a person, product or project. It usually includes footage of an interview and condensed footage of a great performance. Whether it is for an artist, dancer or doctor, the EPK will allow creativity and talent to come to life.

This information, when pitching TV, is useful to the producer or talent booker when making a decision to book musical talent. The EPK is actually the same as a hard copy press kit but it comes alive by showing the artists personality, sense of humor or lack of, and their speaking ability. If it's in your budget to hire someone to produce a quality EPK go for it! If not, wait until you have proper funding. Remember. You must protect your image at all times.

Press clippings

Press clippings are clips of news articles showing proof that the publication printed your work in some form or fashion. It also helps the publicist keep track of their work and proves to the client that work is being done. Larger companies usually retain a clipping service to receive clippings on a monthly basis. Smaller firms will use the service on a per project basis or have a specific person in the office be responsible for collecting the clippings.

Remember to place clippings in order from most current to less current. And only insert the most interesting ones that stand out, preferably the most known publications.

Fact sheet

A one-to-two page bullet-point document giving a brief description of a project, product, event person or service, and any other relevant facts that may be useful to the media.

Press release

A press release is enclosed in the press kit to announce whatever it is you are trying to bring attention to. If you want coverage for a grand opening you will enclose a grand-opening press release. If you want a CD review you will enclose a CD press release. One of the most powerful publicity tactics is to prepare multiple press releases about different newsworthy aspects of your company or product.

Biography or Bio

A biography is mandatory because it tells the recipient about the person, product, company or project. It should be no more than two pages and filled with relevant information. Honestly I could care less what a persons' favorite color is or their favorite restaurant unless it is relevant to the pitch.

A bio should list accolades, contacts and any other information relevant to the press kit. List the main points and keep the fluff to a minimum.

WHY DO I NEED A PRESSKIT?

A press kit is your thirty-second brag. It represents you or your project when you cannot represent in person. With that in mind, you should always put your best foot forward and make a strong introduction--professional but catchy. The full kit could be, and usually is, one of the deciding factors why or why not the media chooses to cover your event, company or product over someone else's.

WHEN DO I SEND THE PRESS KIT?

For event coverage the kit is sent to the media three to six weeks in advance (depending on the media outlet). For a CD review or feature simultaneously with your CD release, the kit should be sent three to four months in advance because most monthly publications work three to four months in advance. Sending your kit too far in advance could result in misplacement of information. Sending the kit too late will result in no coverage at all. It is your responsibility to know the publication deadline.

PRESSKIT ETIQUETTE

You should always send your press kit to the proper recipient. Because the communications field has such a high staff turnover do your research. Call the outlet and get the correct spelling of the recipients name, more importantly make sure they are still employed by the company. If not, find out the current contact and send your package. If this is an unsolicited package call in advance to inform the recipient of its approximate arrival.

DIGITAL PRESS KIT

The most frequently asked questions regarding press kits are "Do I still need to have a paper press kit in today's digital age?" Or "Do I need an online press kit?" The answer is absolutely. You need both.

Today the online press kit is incredibly impressive and there are several advantages from having one: They generate search engine traffic. Reduce distribution costs. Can be accessed immediately by the media. And saves on storage space.

But this doesn't mean you don't need a traditional paper-based press kit. There are many reasons why the traditional press kit is still useful:

- The paper-base kit is very useful at trade shows and conventions. You need this to give to the media and interested persons visiting your booth.

- You need something to send people when they request a copy of your press kit in person.

- You need paper-based kits to hand to people at a press conference.

Although some prefer the hard copy press kit others embrace the electronic version. The fastest way to send a press kit to anyone is via email. Imagine. One click of the button and your press kit is delivered.

You have the choice of downloading material to a CD or sending a file, via email.

Think about it. The cost of a folder, letterhead, CD, envelope, artwork and stamps can be more expensive in the long run. But to be represented across the board, it's to have both.

6

THE PRESS CONFERENCE AND SPECIAL EVENT

A few years ago I represented a major record label whose vice president claimed to be versed in PR but in reality she was the master of confusion. One day she had a bright idea insisting I stage a press conference for a known recording artist who had just been signed to the record label. This recording artist had not even started recording their new CD nor was the artist doing anything news worthy to relay to the media.

Needless to say I decided against a press conference and opted to distribute a press release that conveyed the same information to the media without wasting their time.

A press conference should be used cautiously, since they are somewhat inconvenient for the media. The best way to make enemies with the press is to invite them to a press conference to hear an announcement that could have been sent to them in the form of a press release.

There is only one reason for calling a press conference: The subject demands a question-and-answer format. Or it is necessary to tell the story effectively in person.

Staging a press conference is very detailed and should entail the proper set up. Here are a few things to remember:

- Make sure the news merits a press conference.
- Secure a site to hold your press conference.
- Make sure the site is centrally located with easy access.
- Make sure the site has adequate sound and lighting.
- Make provision for bad weather if the event is outdoors.
- Supply proper lighting if the event is outdoors.

- Apply for permits, if needed.
- Prepare backgrounder sheets or biographies for guests.
- Create invitations or media alerts.
- Secure photographers.

SPECIAL EVENT

Special events come in many forms: building dedication, celebrity appearances, conferences, seminars, grand openings, an introduction of a new product line, CD listening parties and much more.

Planning can start as early as eighteen months in advance, depending on the event. Because the special event is the most visible of PR plans each should be carefully planned and orchestrated for maximum exposure.

Sending press releases, media alerts and press kits, in a timely manner, to the media informing them of the event is crucial. And like any other event the proper way to implement the event is to start at the end and work your way back to day one.

The main objectives to meet, to ensure a successful event, include media exposure and event attendance. The elements involved in staging a special event include:

- Generating pre-event publicity.
- Compiling a target list of attendees.
- Producing publicity material as press kits and invitations.
- Coordinating mailing of invitations.
- Coordinating event displays, parking, security, and the like.
- Securing photographers.
- Securing entertainment when relevant.
- Securing guest speakers when relevant.

And so much more!

Skincare Salon Grand Opening Suggestion

Sometimes the best attraction is something for free. A free skin analysis, free consultation or product coupon. Find out if the salon is being dedicated to someone famous or well known in the area. Will the salon break ground in the winter, in time for a holiday opening or maybe a winter skin-sloughing party preparing the skin for the spring?

Develop an undeniable press kit; packaged in box, that contains fun facts about the company (clientele, testimonials, and product samples, bios for profile stories, current skin trends, and photos of the salon).

Regardless of the event, if you feel you are detailed and can handle stressful situations with a level head, go for it. If not, hire someone who specializes in event planning.

7

UNDERSTANDING THE MEDIA

Your objective as a DIY publicist is to get media attention but before that can happen you must understand the media thoroughly. What some don't realize is that media is being pitched daily by so-called publicists who don't know the format of a particular publication or TV show. It's not unheard of if a TV producer asks, "Have you seen our show?" And what could be more embarrassing is if the publicist answer is, "No." Not only embarrassing but a missed opportunity due to lack of research.

I'll never forget when I was just starting out as a publicist and I called an editor, on the wrong day and time, at a major newspaper and he chewed me out! He explained why he wasn't going to talk to me and how I disrespected his time and that if I knew anything about the newspaper I would have never called him at that particular time. Although I wanted to hang up in his face I stayed on the line and took the abuse. After that day I researched every media outlet before I even attempted to pitch an editor or anyone at any media outlet.

As a DIY publicist you must know what the channels of communication are and how they function.

Selection of the most effective ways to communicate in a public relations campaign is a crucial part of strategy. The DIY publicist must decide which media are most suitable for reaching the desired audiences and attaining the objective. When it comes to publicity there are two audiences: the buying audience and the media audience.

The buying audience is individuals who purchase your product or service. In publicity you must identify your potential customer and find out who is buying what you're selling. If you're a nutritionist your audience will be mainly overweight and health conscious people.

The media audience is members of the press who will publicize your product or services. Once you've identified your buying audience you need to determine which media outlets will reach them. So if the nutritionists' target audience were overweight and health conscious people, the target media would be publications such as *Fitness*, *Shape* and *Weight Watchers*.

Whereas a spa owners target audience would be spa goers and women of leisure, and the target media audience would be *Spa Finder, Towne & Country Travel* and *Spa Magazine*.

A successful DIY publicist must know how the media operate in order to use them effectively in distributing a message. You should understand how to approach each media and to meet its requirements. You'll need to identify the specific audiences you hope to inform and influence. And you must determine which media are best for each publicity campaign.

A few general guidelines for matching media and audience are as follows:

- Print media are the most effective for delivering a message that requires absorption of details by the receiver. Printed information can be read over and over again and kept for reference. Newspapers are the fastest with the most widespread impact. Magazines, while slower, are better directed to special interest audiences such as trades and professional groups. Books take even longer but have a tremendous influence.

- Television has the strongest emotional impact of all media. Its visual power makes situations seem close to the viewer, and personalities on TV create an influence that print media cannot.

- The greatest advantage of radio is flexibility and the ability to reach specific target audiences. Messages can be prepared and broadcast on radio faster than on television. And because there are ten times as many radio stations as TV stations, audience exposure is easier to obtain.

So when is it a good time to contact the media? There is no one format to follow but to make things easier keep a list handy with specific notes for each media contact. This will save you a lot of time and embarrassment. More so, this may save a relationship before it gets started.

Once you have established a relationship with each individual you can begin to set your own rules. To this day I think about my embarrassing and unforgettable experience and still don't know why the guy answered his phone if he was on deadline. Whatever the reason, it taught me a valuable lesson at an early stage in my career.

The media is busy! If you call them on the wrong day expect the worst. You're liable to hear the dial tone or a very annoyed voice on the other end of the phone. Or you may experience blatant rejection as, "No I'm not interested." Which could be avoided if you do your homework. Study your outlets. Know that The Style Network's *Style Star* only feature celebrities and that the ABC network morning talk show *The View* rarely book unknown talent unless they are featuring up and coming comedians on a certain day. And let's not forget radio. There are a lot of morning drive talk shows local, regional and syndicated where the same rules apply. Study your outlets and know them well.

No one is perfect and even the most savvy publicists fall short. As a DIY publicist at all cost try to avoid the following mistakes when working with the media:

- Treating all media--TV and radio, editors and reporters--the same. Learn the different roles and media types, and adjust your media relations accordingly.

- Pitching more than one journalist at a media outlet and not telling them. Don't play this game.

- Pitching exclusives that aren't. Don't.

- Writing press releases that are too long and are not newsworthy. Keep it one page and keep it simple.

- Putting your name in a release and then not being available to take calls. Duh.

- Pitching information or people you can't deliver. Check availabilities before pitching.

- Pitching an outlet blind. Not knowing what the outlet covers can really look bad.

- Not being prepared when pitching verbally. Don't speak to the media unless you're ready.

- Calling on deadline. Once again, do your homework and make sure you know the right times to call.

8

GETTING EXPOSURE
Do You Have What It Takes?

HOW TO LAND A TELEVISION APPEARANCE

Have you ever wondered why or how certain people, specifically non-celebrities, become guests on television talk shows?   Or what they've done to get a spot on *The Oprah Winfrey Show*? Before I was a publicist I would watch TV and wonder why a certain person was sitting in the chair next to David Letterman or why the entertainment news show covered a dancing monkey.

I later found out that, whatever your niche or talent, the media first had to find you or your story newsworthy. Then it had to be something that would be of interest to a large percentage of their viewers and not just your grandmother who is your number one fan.

For example, a married couple renew their vows is an everyday thing. But a married couple who renew their vows bungee jumping off the San Francisco Bridge. Need I say more?

There are numerous ways to get on a television talk show. On the network level there are a few methods used.

Guest appearances on news or talk shows as the *Tonight* and *Today* shows allows one to plug new product, books, films, plays and CD's.

Usually an "A" celebrity like Halle Berry, Denzel Washington, Brad Pitt or Robert Dinero will have no problem getting on a TV talk show to support their new movie. Unfortunately, it's the "B" and "C" celebrities that sometimes don't make the couch.

It's a catch 22. If you're known you sit on the couch, if you're not you don't. In that case it's up to you to be as creative as possible when pitching to make yourself as interesting as possible.

In the event you do not get the couch spot on the first try don't be discouraged. It just means there are a few things you must do. You'll just have to work hard, build your image and become more visible by starting at the local and regional television talk and morning news shows and work your way up to the "big time" shows.

You can start by developing a regional publicity campaign. Let's assume you will be on a promotional tour to support your upcoming CD project.   For every city you visit contact the local TV station and pitch your story for possible coverage. But first, do you have a story? The fact that you're promoting your CD is not always good enough especially if you're a new artist. Promoting your CD and performing at a venue in town is better.

Make sure you have the proper tools before you begin: Performance video footage, an EPK (electronic press kit), and a complete press kit, as well as a pitch letter pertaining to your visit to the city. But before you do anything by all means make sure it's a newsworthy pitch!

Do your homework before the pitch.
- Find out the name and spelling of the person you will be contacting.
- Send your information, in a professional press kit, at least three to four weeks in advance. Sometimes earlier depending on the show.
- Follow up with a call three days after sending your package (depending how the package was sent). If no response, wait a few days and call again. If you can get an email address that's even better.

While a publicist's dream is to confirm appearances on high-visibility network shows such as *The Today Show* and *Good Morning America*, and syndicated national shows like *Live With Regis and Kelly*, cable television opportunities are growing. From BET (Black Entertainment Television) to *E! Entertainment*, cable programming is at a steady rise. Did you know that music-video channels like MTV and VH1 have news spots, and lifestyle segments? And are you aware that *Emeril's* cooking show spotlights bands on occasion? There are so many opportunities in cable that publicists are pitching the networks just as much as they pitch cable shows.

Since we're on the subject of the "other" programming let's not forget public access. Public access is full-time channels that allow local residents to reserve a time slot within the cable's viewing area. The programming is usually local news pertaining to the church, school, art galleries, award ceremonies and the like. Although most view public access as low budget it does have an audience and you have to start somewhere especially if you're trying to get performance and interview footage. It's a win-win situation if it is a quality show. They get their guest and you get your video footage. For free!

If public access makes you nervous local television is an excellent outlet if you have a newsworthy story and feel it will affect or appeal to the local community.

Most every midsize or larger city has at least one local TV station. Local television focuses on local people, places and events. If there is an event outside of the market the only way it will be aired is if it relates to the local area. For instance, if a woman gave birth in a Los Angeles restaurant and a Chicago native, while visiting L.A., helped deliver the baby, the local Chicago evening news will more than likely report the news. On the other hand if you are promoting your project (CD, play, tour) and you are visiting New York to perform at a local club or arena the local news will do anything from having you perform on the show, to sending a camera crew to cover your show, depending on who you are and if there's nothing else going on in the area that weighs heavier. Although this sounds like a full proof plan, you must remember a few things when considering pitching local TV: you are not the only person pitching for the morning or evening spot, your pitch must be stronger and more interesting than the next, and knowing what you're up against, in advance, helps prepare your pitch.

And even if you do all the above there are still other elements to consider: If your story is as good as the next, the one with the strongest visual support (quality video and EPK or electronic press kit) will be placed ahead. Still think you're in the mix? Think again because if the competition's visuals are as equally pleasing as yours the **X** factor kicks in to break the tie. The deciding factor comes down to who has a bigger name, who looks better on camera, and the like. Here's a great example: your singing group will be in Dallas, Texas performing at a popular theater to promote their second CD. The first CD did well with Dallas media and past record sales prove that Dallas really likes the group. Everything is set and you don't see a problem in getting media coverage because nothing else is going on a Tuesday night at 8p.m. Two weeks before you arrive in Dallas, a tour promoter decides to add Dallas, Texas to the schedule at the last minute. No problem right? Maybe not if a circus was coming to town but the tour has four prominent, well-known singers who make your record sales look like chump change. Guess who gets the spot on the local morning show?

HOW TO SECURE PLACEMENT IN A PUBLICATION

Okay. Just in case you don't know by now a publication would be a newspaper, magazine, newsletter, etc.

Getting exposure in a print medium isn't as easy as you may think. As television outlets, publicists are pitching the same limited pages of the same publications, literally at the same time.

For starters know your outlet. Do they have Q&A columns, music reviews and a beauty section in every issue? Do they print issues three to four months ahead? Are they weekly, monthly, bi-monthly or quarterly? How do the editors like receiving material: fax, email or mail?

Feature stories are usually not based on hard breaking news. They take time to develop and usually have a human-interest angle and are longer than news stories. Do you have an interesting story that fits the publication format? Are you an artist who paints with their feet?   Do you have a special skill that makes you stand out from others? Perhaps this is your way to get exposure.

Another way of getting exposure is to write a letter to an editor. This is one of the most read sections in publications. With any luck your background information could be listed with your comment.

A good way to get exposure is to secure a Q&A column in a magazine or newspaper. Are you an expert in your field? Have you written a book? Do you have experience in an area that people want to know about? If so, you may have a chance at having your very own Q&A column. Now that's instant celebrity and credibility.

Think outside the box and be creative. Forget about the norm. Editors and producers like to be the first to publish something different.

9

ONLINE PUBLICITY
The Internet, Web site and E-mail

Since it's inception, the Internet has become the missing link for many people. For the publicist it is a dream come true enabling one to cut down on day-to-day duties, and the cost of mailing and assembling press kits to say the least.

On an average, the cost of a media kit can cost a pretty penny coupled with the amount you'll be sending to the media. Folder prices start at around forty cents each and increase depending on the quality while decent envelopes can cost anywhere from a dollar to two dollars each.

Factor the cost of envelopes and folders with postage being between two to four dollars, depending on the weight of your package, and you could be spending, on an average, five dollars per package. Now multiply that with the number of media outlets you plan to target.

In no way am I saying delete hard copy media kits from your life. Many media outlets still require you to send a full media kit. If you can, sending information through the Internet is definitely an option.

There are several online strategies to get your message to the masses.

Blogging
Blogging is the latest phenomenon to sweep the online world. It has quickly become one of the most popular ways to communicate thoughts, ideas and experiences with the worldwide audience that the Internet provides.
Some people choose to blog about their favorite sports teams, politics, their

personal trials and tribulations, religion, technology, their hopes, their fears, and some even use blogging as an outlet for fictional writing. The best thing about blogging is that there are no rules. So whatever you're thinking blog it!

Online Publications

Most online publications are an extension of the paper magazine with a twist. It has a plethora of information separate from the magazine but it also highlights information from the main publication. For example, Essence Magazine also publishes Essence.com. It stays in tune with their paper magazine but may feature a recording artist or actor that the main magazine did not.

Online publications will more than likely feature "B" or "C" celebrities faster than paper magazines.

E-Zine

An E-zine is an electronic magazine delivered via email. Most are like printed magazines and rely on advertising to support them. Some are sent to subscribers only. Nonetheless this is a great way to get your message out to a mass audience.

This is a great way to collect clippings at a fast pace. The turnaround is faster and you can usually go online and print your feature to add to your press kit.

Online Newsletters

A newsletter is a special timely report on a single subject. It is a personalized, concise statement from an expert or person thoroughly familiar with a specialized field. You don't have to be a famous business consultant to produce a newsletter.

Online newsletters are a great for informing the masses with information usually on a specific area of interest. Some are general but most focus on a specific field.

You can find newsletters on music, spa's, women-interest, technology, business, public relations and other topics.

One way to get your name or product "out there" is to create your own newsletter and send it to your specific media and industry contacts on a quarterly basis. This is a great way to become an expert in your field. If you write songs distribute a newsletter on songwriting. If you specialize in skin care send a monthly newsletter to doctors, skin care salons and people suffering from acne.

The most important aspect of creating a successful newsletter is the market. You need to research who will want the subscription and how to get it to them. If you have a special interest that has a broad following, you might find that a newsletter will be readily accepted and thrive. It's important that the information in your newsletter is current, and cannot easily be found elsewhere. It is equally important that information contained in the newsletter motivate readers to follow the advice and want more. What are the latest trends? Where are the best trade shows? Who are the hottest music producers? How do I write a song? There is an endless need for specific knowledge in every field. Since there is a high standard of competition within every aspect of our modern life, people search for ways to be in the know, and use that information effectively. One of the reasons why a newsletter could be a way for you to get the notoriety you need. And possibly start a business in the process.

Web site

Having a web site is ingenious! There are so many things you can do with a web site. You can sell your product, services and the like. You can attach your newsletter to it making it available for thousands of readers. Other sites can also link to your site, bringing you even more business. The opportunities are endless.

10
RESEARCH

An effective public relations campaign is a process, and it starts with research. Research will aid you in meeting your objectives in your publicity campaign. You can't begin the process of a PR campaign if you have no information. Think about it. Can you write a press release about something you know nothing about? Could you intelligently speak on a foreign subject if you are not familiar?

The role of research in public relations is vital and is used for many reasons. Before attempting to create a plan you should know why you're creating it, who you want to reach, and what is the expected outcome.

Research prevents you from wasting time. Recently an independent record company attempted to hire my company to secure media coverage for their new recording artist. By sending them a very detailed questionnaire I was able to conclude that they were not ready to retain a publicist or PR firm at the time.

Although the record was recorded, mixed, packaged and ready to go, the label had not secured distribution, a radio or retail representative or marketing plan. My suggestion was for them to connect the missing links before seeking a PR firm. Had I not asked questions or sent the questionnaire a lot of time would have been wasted.

Another incident was when I had to create and distribute a press release about a client who was appearing on a national TV show to discuss their annual conference. Since this was a new client I was not aware of all the conference details. I called the client's assistant on several occasions with no response. Time was running out so I went online and tried to get as much information I could find, about the conference, to create a press release. I then called the TV station's producer to reconfirm the date and time the client would appear on the show as well as the airdate.

I then had enough information to create a well thought-out press release announcing when the client would be on the show and why. I also had enough time to distribute the press release to various mediums for coverage and several audiences to ensure viewing.

Research is imperative when communicating effectively. It is necessary to know your audience and know your product. Once you understand the audience-attitudes, concerns, frustrations, likes, dislikes- you will be better able to create messages that appeal directly to them. The more tailored your message, the better chance of reaching your audience. A good way to find out how your target audience is thinking is to ask. Well, ask in a more formal, structured, professional manner. A survey is a good tool to use especially if you want to know what your audience is thinking or if they like or dislike a certain product. By getting almost instant feedback from your audience you have a very good idea what direction your campaign should go and what type of changes, if any, you'll need to make.

Research takes place everyday in public relations whether it's scanning newspapers or television programs to view their formats, or surfing the Internet for detailed information about an event. It can be as simple as bringing a group of friends together for a book read or CD listening party, or as complex as a national poll to gauge public opinion.

Research can accomplish a number of objectives:
- Reveal public concerns before they transpire into a full-scale explosion
- Help pretest a product, and get the kinks out, before implementing a campaign

- Measure true opinions of various groups
- Help explore attitudes of groups so that messages can be structured to better serve the consumer.

Questions to be asked before conducting a research will help you determine the extent of the research that is needed. Some of the following questions may include:

- What is the problem?
- What kind of information is needed?
- How will the results of research be used?
- What specific public(s) should be researched?
- What research techniques will be used?
- How will the research results be analyzed?
- How much will it cost?

Remember research is imperative before any public relations process can be mapped out in an effort to create an effective campaign or even to create a press release.

11

PLANNING THE ACTION
THE PROCESS

Now that you are familiar with the communication tools needed to function in public relations, and have an understanding of how the tools work together, it's time to plan the action. A public relations campaign is the process used to ensure proper results. Although not the easiest task to implement, having an understanding and direction is half the battle.

A public relations campaign or publicity plan should not be a hit or miss action. When a problem arises, and they do, it is irresponsible to attack it randomly, in hopes of hitting the target. Rather a successful campaign consists of a series of basic steps.

The process starts with a definition of the problem or situation and ends with a solution or an assessment of the results.

The public relations process is a method for solving problems or taking advantage of an opportunity. Not to be confusing, a problem is not looked upon as a negative in all public relations cases. But because each public relations program has to have an outcome or solution to be successful, the word "problem" is used.

The method has four phases: research, objectives, programming, and evaluation. Each element may be modified by the demands of the different audiences or publics.

The research phase of the process involves identifying and learning about three key elements: (1) a **client** or company that has (2) a **problem** or potential problem to be solved, which involves (3) one or more of its **audiences** or publics.

The second phase of the process involves the setting of **objectives** for a program to solve the problem. This part describes what you want to achieve for example, to change the attitudes or to sell product.

The third phase of the process consist of designing a **program** to accomplish the objectives. This is where you take action by sending a press release, faxing media alerts and so on.

The last phase of the process involves follow-up **evaluation.** The evaluation is based on whether or not the objectives, in phase two, were achieved. Did the program change attitudes or modify opinions? If not, back to the drawing board because the publicity campaign was not a success.

A typical media relation's process:

R – research – Do your homework. Know the background of the client or product.

O – objectives – List what you want the outcome to be.

P – programming – Implement the objectives with action.

E – evaluation – Were your objectives met?

The four-stage process is useful in all aspects of public relations. In media relations it involves establishing a favorable working relationship between the publicist and the media.

The most important aspect of research for a media relations campaign is the preparation of up-to-date lists of media contacts. The objective in media relations is to obtain favorable media coverage for your event, product or service. An absolute must for a media relation process is the understanding of the media outlets' audiences (know what consumers read and watch the media outlets you are targeting) in other words know the format of every outlet you plan to pitch.

Evaluation of media relations always refers back to the stated objectives; however, the effectiveness of media relations always comes down to media placement. Was the desired media placement obtained?

12
THE PUBLICITY PLAN
The Blueprint

To get the most out of your publicity plan it must be accurate and detailed. Just as an entrepreneur needs a business plan to improve their chances of success, the DIY publicist must follow a publicity plan for the same reason.

Depending on how detailed your campaign will be, it is wise to begin implementing your plan at least nine months before you introduce your product or service to your audience.

Depending on your product the first three months should be dedicate to researching media outlets, writing pitch letters and press releases, creating or updating biographies, designing brochures, press kits and newsletters, and pitching the media.

The next three months should focus on distributing press releases, scheduling interviews, securing event coverage and media placement.

The last three months should be dedicated to reconfirming print and television placement, coordinating the guest list (if you're having an event), sending reminders as "save the date," sending invitations, reconfirming interviews, and ensuring that all objectives are being met.

The plan should start with a specific introduction stating what you plan to do. As you implement your plan you are bound to make changes. Don't be alarmed this is normal because the more you work from your plan the more you will experience different opinions from the press, advice from comrades and the like. Not that you have to take their advice but keep an open mind.

INCORPORATE EDITORIAL CALENDARS INTO YOUR PUBLICITY CAMPAIGN

Submitting a press release to media outlets whenever something new comes up can certainly produce results, but there is still more you can do. There is a tool that publicists depend on for a better chance of landing media placement - the editorial calendar. Editorial calendars are schedules of topics or features a publication plans to cover for a particular week, month, quarter or year. Most editorial calendars are posted on a publication's Web site.

Again, since most publications work anywhere from six weeks to six months in advance of the publication date, you should check with the publication to see how far in advance you should submit your news for consideration. Editorial calendars can also assist in the selection of the news angle. For instance, if you discover that a particular publication will be featuring articles on new recording artists or a restaurant with the best French toast, turn it into a press release and submit it. You'll definitely have a jump start on your pitch.

Keep in mind that some publications simply do not have editorial calendars.

Publicity Plan for Media Relations Campaign
INTRODUCTION

Media coverage will be secured for the author of "Do-It-Yourself Publicity" from January 2006 to December 2006 through various mediums.

The next heading is goal. This statement should hone in on the overall plan somewhat more than the introduction.

GOAL

To implement a public relations campaign responsible for generating publicity to elevate local, regional and national awareness for the book and author.

The objective is the next heading. Each objective should be stated with an action word. For example, conceive, secure, enhance, etc.

OBJECTIVE

To convince the consumer to purchase the book online and in stores.

TARGET AUDIENCE

The target audience is whom you are trying to appeal to by demographics and psychographics. Demographics are characteristics such as age, income, education, geography, gender, and occupation. Psychographics examine the behavior, lifestyle, and psychological make-up of your potential customers; for instance, their hobbies, favorite vacation spots, political views, and values. In order to advertise and sell effectively it is wise to know both the demographics and psychographics of your target audience.

RESEARCH

The research process for a PR plan includes investigation of the client, of the opportunity or problem that accounts for communication with the media, and of the various audiences to be targeted for the PR effort.

Client Research

First you should be familiar with the background of the client or organization. Special attention must be given to past and present relations with media representatives. Has the client had negative or positive news coverage in the past? Has there been any coverage at all? Does the client have media strengths or weaknesses or any newsworthy topics to discuss?

Opportunity Research

The second step of research involves determining the reason for the program. Has an opportunity presented itself for good news coverage?

Audience Research

The final step of research is identifying the appropriate media and their audience to target. These media fall into two broad categories, mass and specialized.

Mass media

Local – print publications, newspapers, magazines, television stations and radio stations

National – print publications, broadcast networks, wire services

Specialized media

Local – trade, association, industry, membership, women-interest and ethnic publications and specialized broadcast programs and stations (Christian Broadcasting Network and HGTV)

National – National ethnic publications (Essence, Ebony, Xii Magazine), national trade, industry, and association publications (Hollywood Reporter, Billboard, Spin, Variety, BRE)

Once you have the media categories prepare a complete media list and include the following:

- Type and size of audience reached by each media outlet
- Type of material used by the media outlet – feature material, interviews, photos, DVD
- Name and title of appropriate editor, director, reporter, or staff writer
- Deadlines for each media contact—monthly, weekly, daily, morning,

afternoon, evening, date, day or hour

Each media outlet has its own unique set of departments and editorial staff, with particular requirements for submitting material.

OBJECTIVES

Your objectives should be very specific, measurable, and attainable within the determined timeframe, and should compliment your marketing plan and the main goal of increasing revenue.

List the objectives that you want your public relations campaign to accomplish such as enhance company image, create awareness, generate positive word-of-mouth, broaden your customer base, etc.

Two types of objectives for most P.R. plans are impact and output.

<u>Impact Objectives</u>

Impact objectives represent the desired outcomes of changing the attitudes and behaviors of your target audience. They include statements as these:

- To increase favorable media coverage
- To enhance the client's credibility with media
- To convince the consumer to purchase a client's product

<u>Output Objectives</u>

Output objectives refer to the efforts made through action. They include statements as theses:

- To provide newsworthy stories about the client
- To coordinate interviews with the client
- To act as a spokesperson on the client's behalf

The next heading is strategy. It consists of the actual implementation of the publicity campaign.

STRATEGY

Summarize how you plan to implement your public relations objectives. Strategies should include the broad who, what, when, and where of accomplishing your objectives.

- Send written information (press release) to media announcing book
- Pitch and service all press material to solicit coverage
- Set up electronic and print interviews
- Set up local and regional book signings

After the objectives are listed it would be logical to list media outlets you will contact or pitch in implementing the publicity campaign. The client or product will dictate the media list you will create. Regional newspapers, national magazines, specialized publications i.e., women-interest, technology trades, music trades, and the like. Only list those that match the format of your product or client. In other words, don't pitch a book if the newspaper has no literature editor or book review section. If you own a hair salon, pitch beauty outlets. If you sing gospel music, pitch faith-based outlets.

TACTICS

Determine the specific action you will take to support your strategies and meet your objectives such as press release distribution, what level of publicity, what type of special event, if personal appearances are relevant, etc. Every tactic should include a deadline and a budget.

The publicity plan is substantial as it relates to a successful campaign. Remember to do your research and investigate your media outlets to create a thorough plan that works.

The Publicity Budget

No one likes to discuss money when it's coming out of his or her pocket but if they expect to have a successful PR event or campaign it's going to cost.

In planning a campaign and setting objectives you must factor in the cost and start by including fixed expenditures.

Basically, your direct cost will usually include but not limit the following:

Brochures

Postage

Telephone

Faxing

Envelopes

Flyers

Paper

Printing

Photos

Retouching of photos

Art work

Postcards

Film

Press kit folders

Graphics

There are several ways to get around some of the expenses. One way to get good help for free is to visit your local university graduate program. I'm sure you will find a photojournalism major or a graphic design major willing to do your work as their senior project. It's a win-win situation. They're certainly not going to mess up because they need to graduate. And you get their best work for your portfolio.

There are also wholesale paper companies and printing companies. Or being the savvy businessperson you are (I know because you purchased this book) try bartering. I find bartering to be a breath of fresh air. Just don't barter too much because you won't have time for your own project.

Your publicity campaign will generally cost more than anticipated so always add at least a 15 percent padding to be safe.

Remember. If the cost of a campaign exceeds the value of its objectives, the effort is not a success.

13
EVALUATION
Measuring Your Results

Just when you think it's over it's not. The last step in any publicity campaign is measuring the results or evaluating your efforts.

There are several methods for evaluating a publicity campaign including audience acceptance, measurement of message exposure, attitude change, and the like. Whether it's you or the client the most common questions asked after the end of a campaign is were the objectives met? If not, why? What worked? What didn't? How can the plan be tailored to better meet your needs?

In PR, results are measured by whether or not you met the objectives listed in the publicity campaign. Did you get coverage in certain publications? Were you able to change the attitude of the consumer towards a certain product? Did you increase awareness of a certain recording artist?

Collecting news clippings, video clips and magazine articles shows PR results. You can retain a clipping service or do it yourself. But if you're reading this book I'm guessing you'll opt to do it yourself.

Relying on an editor to send you clippings can be nerve racking. For one, it's not their job but if you have a good rapport they will. When they have time.

Suggestions:
- Subscribe to the main media outlets you will pitch on occasion
- Order the issue of the publication you will appear in
- Hang out at the news stand and read magazines from cover to cover

If you need a copy of a television talk show bring your VHS to the station and ask if they will tape the show. Most shows will do this with no problem.

Not all objectives will be met. Not because you didn't do your job but because that's life. I have had the pleasure of having egg on my face a numerous amount of times. There was a time when I secured, or so I thought I secured a feature for a client, in a major publication, only to find out it didn't make the cut. How did I find out? The client eagerly waited at the newsstand for the delivery of the publication and when they did not find their feature I received a very disappointed call. Turns out the editor had a change of heart, at the last minute before going to print, and didn't care to let me know. I know it's not right but it happens all the time.

14
ASPECTS OF PUBLIC RELATIONS

Now that you have some insight you may be interested in pursuing a career in PR. There are so many aspects of public relations but I have listed my favorites for your review.

MEDIA RELATIONS

A publicist who specializes in media relations practices the art of "pitching". The main objective is to get results—meaning favorable print and television coverage for their client. In media relations, the publicist becomes very familiar with the media and must know the format of various mediums. As a DIY publicist, it is your job to know when a staff member leaves a particular media outlet and where they land.

Publicists who practice media relations create programs to sell to the media. Although it may sound simple, successful media relations depend on building a genuine rapport with the target audience (editors, reporters, TV producers) while giving them newsworthy information they can build on. The press release is the key to media relations, while media contacts keep it pushing. No contacts no plan.

- Typical tasks of media relations plans include:
- Developing news and feature stories for print and electronic media
- Developing press releases for media distribution
- Gaining favorable product review
- Staging media tours, media events and press conferences
- Positioning clients as an expert in their field by securing a column in a monthly magazine or on a daily radio spot
- Arranging press tours

PERSONAL AND ENTERTAINMENT PR

Personal and Entertainment PR are somewhat synonymous. Public relations firms or publicists specializing in personality buildup and personal PR spend most of their time pitching clients to the media. They keep the media aware of client activities by distributing news worthy press releases. When Tiger Woods announced his engagement his personal publicist sent out a press release for immediate release. When Julia Roberts became pregnant more than likely her publicist sent a press release as well. Unfortunately in some cases the media gets a hold of the information before the publicist can send it to them. When this happens the outcome could be a disaster and the publicist will have to prepare for damage control.

A prime example of entertainment PR is when you see Halle Berry or Brad Pitt on the cover of entertainment or trade magazines and simultaneously as guests on television talk shows they have a movie releasing soon.

Other duties of an entertainment publicist include: making follow-up phone calls to the media encouraging stories and/or interviews, creating news, creating photo opportunities, shepherding clients to appearances, and much more.

COMMUNITY RELATIONS

Community relations is linked to image and it is the publicist job to bring the company or corporation's name to the public in a positive way. For a corporation the easiest way to become a pillar in the community and be in good standing is to support poverty programs, minority programs, community programs and especially donate to a charity.

A great example of a community relations campaign is when *Tasai Salon & Day Spa* of Scripps Ranch, California donated their time and earnings to the victims of the horrible fire in San Diego, California in November 2003. Although their main concern was helping their neighbors in time of need, they became instant heroes in the community because of their selfless contribution to the community. Thus, gaining publicity for the spa.

PUBLIC AFFAIRS

Public affairs specialist tasks involve lobbying and gathering intelligence on the activities of federal and state legislative and executive bodies and regulatory agencies.

Duties of the pubic affairs specialist include:
- Writing and distributing press releases and lobbying support materials.
- Organizing meetings with Congress members, commissioners, staff members and administrators.
- Analyzing various proposed and existing legislation and regulations.
- Keeping abreast of all public policy issues.

EMERGENCY PUBLIC RELATIONS/DAMAGE CONTROL

Because of the nature of emergencies it is difficult to plan objectives. As a DIY publicist, in an emergency situation, it is your duty to 1.provide accurate information to all targeted audiences. 2.maintain a positive image 3.demonstrate concern for the safety of lives.

Other areas that I find most interesting include sports PR, consumer relations, investor relations, member relations, and employee relations.

15

PUBLIC RELATIONS & THE LAW

In a matter of weeks a former employee of *Pc Public Relations & Management, Inc.* was able to turn what I thought would be an easy task into an almost disaster. My company just completed a project for a major company that included a new press kit with biographies, press releases and a new company logo. After we researched and proofed all literature with a fine-tooth comb I decided to look over everything one final time. As I began proofing I found a few quotes from the client that had not been fully checked out and confirmed as truth. It turns out that this particular quote, had I not seen it, would have made my company a prime target for a libel suit.

Before you attempt to practice PR it would behoove you to understand the responsibility a publicist has as it relates to the law and the media.

In order for a publicist or an acting publicist to do their job well they must know the laws and government regulations that affect the content and distribution of a message.

A publicist can be held liable for malpractices as (1) using a copyrighted article or cartoon without permission, (2) writing a press release that makes false claims about a product, or (3) using a photo without proper authorization.

Because publicists are considered the spokesperson for a product or company the impact of what they say is taken very serious.

Libel And Slander

It is the responsibility of the publicist to make sure that a company brochure;

document, publication or speech does not defame anyone.

Defamation is a published or spoken false statement that damages a person's reputation. A written defamation constitutes *libel* and an oral defamation, *slander*.

Most libel suits are directed against newspapers, magazines, and broadcast or electronic media when an individual feels that a false statement has damaged their reputation or character. A well-known actress successfully sued the National Inquire for printing a story that implied she was having an affair with a married man.

Libel and slander suits have also been filed against company officials when they send out news releases or make false statements that damage someone's reputation.

Fair Comment And Criticism

An individual or even a company criticizing another corporate body for poor products or terrible service usually does so under the protection of what is phrased *fair comment and criticism*. This is the same concept that theater and music critics use when they attack a play or a concert. In short, companies and individuals who voluntarily show their goods to the public for sale or consumption are subject to "fair comment," whether good or bad. Although everyone has the right to comment on matters of public interest and concern, it should be done with honest purpose and not have cruel intent.

The Public Figure Concept

What constitutes a *public figure* is another concept that publicists should also know from the standpoint of answering press inquiries. A public figure is a person that is usually in the limelight such as athletes, actors, government officers, and political candidates. Unfortunately these figures usually have trouble winning suits for libel, slander, and invasion of privacy. On the other hand, a company executive who has not sought the limelight is more likely to be considered a private citizen, with a better chance of winning a suit.

Photo Releases

A photo release is important to have if a person protests that their picture was used without permission.

A publicist releasing photos to the media should have a file with available information with the source of the picture and date taken, copyright information, and signed releases from subjects in photos.

This information will guarantee proper use of photos and reduce the risk of lawsuits. A record of the date taken will help eliminate the use of a photo that is no longer appropriate for press releases or company brochures. This is especially good when a person's photo is being used and they are deceased, or a company has moved but the media is still printing the former office photo.

The copyrighting of a picture by a photographer may mean that a company cannot use it again unless the photographer gives permission or receives payment.

For the most part a publicist doesn't need to worry about getting a signed release if the person gives consent by posing for a photo and is told how it will be used. This is particularly true for a photo accompanying a press release.

Photography And Artwork

The copyright law makes it clear that freelance and commercial photographers retain ownership of the image in a picture unless they specifically agree, in writing, to surrender that right. In other words, these photographers own all negatives, and they can negotiate with business regarding the use of a picture. In any event, a publicist should always tell the photographer, up front, how the photo will be used. Arrangements and fees can then be determined for one-time use, unlimited use, or the payment of royalties every time the picture is used.

Unfortunately there is much confusion or neglect in honoring a photographer's copyright. All the same, it is the responsibility of the publicist, or whoever hired them, to give compensation and/or recognition for a photographer's work.

Other important laws the publicist should be aware include: fair use versus infringement, employee rights, ownership of ideas, trademarks, the Federal Trade Commission (FTC) and the Securities and Exchange Commission (SEC).

IT'S A WRAP!

Now you're ready to apply what you've learned to create and implement a successful publicity campaign. Who am I kidding? If it were that easy I'd be out of a job. I can't tell you how many mistakes I made when I first began practicing PR. But as anything else, practice makes perfect. So be expected to read this book a few times and refer to it often considering this is your first stab as a DIY publicist. But the more you read and practice the better you will get.

Don't be discouraged if your campaign is not a success the first try. It takes practice, hard work and tenacity but it will pay off when you are able to measure your results. As long as you're consistent, follow up appropriately and follow the rules you should do fine.

Publicists have various styles of writing, pitching and planning events. This book gives you the basics to get started. Once you get the hang of it you will more than likely add your twist to meet your liking.

Let this book be your guide and refer to it as much as possible until you know it from cover to cover.

It's a wrap!

WRITING SAMPLES

APPENDIX 1

Biography Samples

Pitch Letter Samples

Press Release Samples

Media Alert Samples

Fact Sheet Samples

APPENDIX 2

Business Letters

PR Case Problems

DIY PR Pop Quiz

Media Resources

Public Relations Organizations

PRODUCT BIOGRAPHY

Benaleigh Custom Jewelry

"It's for the versatile, fashion forward woman who dares to be different," said Brenda Caddell, designer of benaleigh custom jewelry design one of a kind semi-precious gems. "When I began the design process I thought about what type of woman would look great in my designs and at the same time make my designs look good."

benaleigh custom designs was crated after Caddell became frustrated with stores that didn't carry the type of jewelry she was looking for and because she dares to be different. "I dress very eccentric and I like to accessorize with different pieces to go with my wardrobe," she said. "Designing my own jewelry line gives me the freedom to be as creative as I want and always have a piece to compliment my wardrobe."

Caddell was excited to implement her vision because she realized she could make one-of-a-kind pieces that would stand out from the rest and she was embarking on yet another exciting creative adventure.

She began by making chokers and necklaces for her friends and family. Shortly after she would receive requests from people who saw her pieces enhancing someone's neck. "I started taking orders once a month, then twice a month and before I knew it I was giving private showings at the homes of some notable Hollywood figures."

-more-

As a musician/songwriter and prior language arts teacher she is no stranger to creativity and often compares the feeling of designing jewelry to music.

"I compare semi precious stones like kunzite, rose quartz or peridots to several bars of syncopated musical notes combined with slurred legatos, staccatos or repetitive phrases," she said. "Like music, the stones continuously tug at my creativity. When this happens there is no rest until I have completed the composition or in this case a beautiful piece of semi-precious gemmed jewelry."

benaleigh custom jewelry designs continue to delight and surprise their customers with vibrant one-of-a-kind designs for women and young girls.

# # #

BUSINESS-OWNER BIOGRAPHY

JOAN JACKSON
Tasai Salon & Day Spa
Biography

An avid connoisseur of some of the most prestigious day spas and resort spas in the world, coupled with an immense background in customer service and sales, Joan Jackson, an aggressive businesswoman has always been ahead of the game especially when it was time to open the doors to her latest venture - *Tasai Salon & Day Spa.*

As owner of *Tasai Salon & Day Spa*, a full-service salon and day spa offering complete body and skin treatments and the finest services and products in San Diego, California, she prides herself and staff on consistent quality customer service.

"Although my college degree is in word processing and data processing, the beauty industry is a field I've been researching for several years," she explained. "My travels have taken me to spas from Barcelona to Arizona and with each visit I became more intrigued and eager to open my own salon & day spa."

The wife of 15-year-veteran football player John Jackson, and mother of two, Joan Jackson is the epitome of energy.

"I've always been used to juggling at least four things at one time," she said. "I

-more-

enjoy helping and working with people and putting them at ease."

In fact she and her husband John are such giving people they appeared on "The Oprah Winfrey Show" and brought $5,000.00 worth of coins in a wheelbarrow for Oprah's Angel Network that sends one child from each state in the U.S. to college.

Jackson has numerous responsibilities aside from caring for her family. She runs the John and Joan Jackson Foundation, an organization geared towards helping kids reach a higher level in education. She travels at least four times per month, runs the salon & day spa and gets dinner on the table in a timely manner.

Super woman? Some would say. But Joan Jackson takes it all in stride, prays everyday and keeps her faith in God.

"My joy comes from knowing that God is in my life and with God everything is possible."

Jackson further explained that Tasai was built as an escape for people. "When our clients step into our salon & day spa, we want them to forget about their problems and let us provide a quality and relaxing environment."

When describing Joan Jackson one word will not suffice. She is a resourceful, spiritual, organized, professional, warm, thoughtful, generous, encouraging woman of God.

# # #

MUSIC CD BIOGRAPHY

"OUT OF EDEN"
LOVE, PEACE, AND HAPPINESS
BIOGRAPHY

Sibling members Lisa Kimmey, Andrea Kimmey-Baca, and Danielle Kimmey have proven themselves as members of the seven-figure club (million plus copies sold), and have shared the stage with such icons as Destiny's Child, the Pointer Sisters, CeCe Winans and Kirk Franklin.

As their combined album sales continue to move well beyond the one million mark "Love, Peace and Happiness," the trio's fifth album to release February 10, 2004, exhibits energetic songs that exude inspiration and feed the soul. The group's signature harmonies and precise production cater to a diverse audience and showcase their love for entertaining, inspiring and blessing.

Throughout the project they deliver 12 songs with flavorful ingredients that make for an undeniable recipe of R&B, hip-hop and inspirational pop driven songs with a twist of soul.

The title track "Love, Peace and Happiness," the first single and video, illustrates excitement and enjoyment and takes the listener on a rhythmic ride that keeps them wanting more. With true to life hip-hop lyrical content, the youth-driven *Soldiers* and *Make Way* continues to build the momentum and sends the message that it's okay to be a Christian and have fun. Both *It's You* and *Shoulda Listened* are triple

-more-

threats. They have strong advisory messages, showcase soulful R&B laid back beats and reel you in to praise God. *What's Your Secret* and *Coulda Been Me* display life situations over mid-tempo melodies that make you instantly think about your existence. The CD closes appropriately with *Sincerely*, a song that thanks God for everything He has done while declaring that He didn't have to do anything.

"This album is like a couple of chapters away from our last one," said Lisa, the eldest of the siblings, and the group's supervising producer and lead songwriter. "We saw what we had done with our last album and definitely took it up few notches." "We experimented with some different sounds and vibes and just kept working until we got it right."

The progression of the group's musical and spiritual drive is gradually revealed on each project. " I think the growth has to happen before you work on a project and the album reflects that," said Lisa. "If you're not spending time with God and growing in Him before you get in the studio, it's impossible to manufacture it." "As far as our musical growth," she continues. "We constantly try to expose ourselves to all kinds of music and are always open to hearing something new. I think that keeps us growing."

From the legendary gospel artist Shirley Caesar to R&B artist Monica, the group's diversity has given them the opportunity to share the stage with a variety of artists.

In addition, their ever-growing vision has positioned them in many high-profile situations from opening slots on major arena tours to placing songs in such screen successes as Eddie Murphy's "Dr. Doolittle," Christina Aguilera's *Diary*, *The Chris Rock Show*, and a guest appearance on the primetime UPN show *Moesha* (starring Brandy). Likewise, the group has scored key radio success, major video rotation on BET, and several major magazine features and cover stories, including Upscale,

Black Elegance, Sound and Spirit (BMG), Hype Hair, Sister 2 Sister, BRE, and Gospel Today.

According to the platinum-selling sister act, this album is probably their most fun, lighthearted ever. "We take our audience everywhere," said Lisa. "We take them to church, to the club, to the live show, to the altar, to the Word, and to the journal. We just take a ride. Still there's depth in what we're saying and how we say it. The message is always in our music."

Out of Eden has created a very diverse album. And although it is socially and spiritually conscious, the light-hearted and fun side creates a steady balance. "This project is like a giant exhale," said Lisa. "There is so much going on in the world and while we don't want to make light of that, we want to give people something to help them get through the stress and anxiety of life. We want people to remember that we do have a life in Christ that deserves celebration. This album is like a fun, much deserved vacation."

#

MUSIC CD BIOGRAPHY

PASTOR SHIRLEY CAESAR
BIOGRAPHY
"I KNOW THE TRUTH"

San Francisco Examiner critic James Kelton said, "The energy transmitted between her and her audience makes most rock'n'roll fanaticism seem like empty piety." A quote that still stands true today for the energetic 11-time Grammy Award-winning artist Shirley Caesar.

Whether mingling with Oprah Winfrey, shooting a film with Beyonce or performing for the President of The United States, she continues to record albums that not only win multiple awards but also touch individuals in unexplainable measures.

A woman who has always exhibited unparalleled charisma, who could have, long ago, retired and rested on her many successes, does it again.

On September 6, 2005 Caesar will release her 41st CD "I Know The Truth"-the first to be released on her new record label *Shu-Bel Records*-distributed through *Artemis Gospel* (formerly known as Light Records), to include 12 tracks with a variety of styles including a twist of hip hop, church, and quartet where she undoubtedly brings her signature energetic powerhouse vocals with an abundance of love and encouragement.

"We at Artemis Gospel are honored to partner with Pastor Shirley Caesar and her

-more-

label *Shu-Bel Records* and consider it a privilege to be chosen as her label home," said Phillip White, former GM of Light Records now President of *Artemis Gospel*.

"To begin a new label with an artist of the caliber of Pastor Caesar is a dream situation that few label executives ever get to experience."

Just as people listened to her past recordings and were encouraged, "I Know The Truth" continues her philosophy and combines music with ministry to convey her messages.

The unexpected surprise is Stellar and Dove award-winning recording artist Tonéx who joined Caesar in the studio collaborating on "I Know The Truth" where Caesar actually raps.

"Working with Pastor Caesar was nothing short of amazing", said Tonéx. Not only is she young and hip, she wanted to do the hard stuff in hip-hop that I didn't expect to happen. I have wanted to put her in my world for about five years now and I spoke it prophetically a long time ago. I still can't believe that it's really manifesting!"

Other standout songs include "Every Day is Like Mother's Day," in memory of Caesar's mother, and "Jail Bird," a country song about a man on death row who commits himself to God.

Overall, Caesar takes her listeners on a joyous ride showing versatility while her usual energy uplifts and encourages.

"The project itself is vintage Shirley Caesar and offers a few things a little different from the norm for her," said producer Sanchez Harley. "The industry

-more-

should get ready, cause Pastor Caesar is still here."

Earning numerous accolades including 11Grammys, 13 Stellar Awards, 18 Dove Awards, an induction into the Gospel Music Hall of Fame, and recently honored at Oprah Winfrey's Legend's Ball for her contributions to the arts and entertainment, Caesar has surpassed her wildest dreams.

She has successfully recorded forty albums and performed duets with extraordinary vocalists as Patti Labelle, Gladys Knight, Faith Evans and Destiny's Child Michelle Williams enabling her to effectively bridge the gap between R&B and Gospel music.

Indeed a living legend, Caesar has made several notable appearances including a series of commercials for MCI Communications, the televised Live from Disney World Night of Joy, the Gospel According to VH-1, a White House performance for George Bush, and a speech on the Evolution of Gospel Music to the US Treasury Department.

She completed her third sold-out run on Broadway, starring in "Born To Sing," the third installment of the "Mama I Want to Sing" trilogy. She played New York's Madison Square Garden in the hit gospel musical, "This Is My Song," with Cissy Houston and Tramaine Hawkins. She has also been involved with four major motion picture soundtracks, including Whitney Houston's "The Preacher's Wife," the John Singleton film "Rosewood," and acting roles with Warner Brothers Films' "Why Do Fools Fall In Love," and Paramount Pictures "The Fighting Temptations" with Cuba Gooding, Jr. and Beyonce' Knowles.

While the music industry keeps her busy, she always finds her way back to assume her pastoral duties, at Mt. Calvary Word of Faith in North Carolina, where her messages of encouragement and peace are heard throughout the community.

Shirley Caesar is the essence of inspiration and vitality--a global sensation. For more information, go to www.shirleycaesar.com.

-30-

RECORDING ARTIST BIO

DAYNA CADDELL
URBAN INSPIRATIONAL SINGER/SONGWRITER

Whether wowing a crowd at an ASCAP event or having one of the top-selling duos in the industry backing her on stage, singer/songwriter Dayna Caddell is an anointed singer who real music lovers and worshippers can appreciate. No padding, no artificial flavoring, just God-given talent and a sincere love for the Lord.

Her voice, described by a sound engineer, "is like a warm cup of cocoa oozing down your throat on a cold winter day."

As a child she was constantly surrounded by music. Her father, a former recording studio owner and road manager for jazz fusion group **"Weather Report"**, and her godfather, the late Latin jazz percussionist **Willie Bobo,** exposed her to countless jam sessions and concerts that often took place within their home. But what truly encouraged her to belt out that first note were the sounds of Rufus & Chaka Khan blaring throughout her home constantly by her eldest sister Brenda. Before she could recite her ABC's she was emulating various artists and thoroughly absorbing it all.

"I am the product of rock, hip-hop, soul, R&B, jazz and gospel all wrapped up in one. I was blessed to have experienced a variety of music and talent from the day I was born. I exude music. It's so much of who I am!"

Her versatility has afforded her the opportunity to sing background vocals for

Diana Ross for the 1997 Super bowl, and appear on *The Tonight Show With Jay Leno* singing background for pop artist **Bisou Phillips**.

In the Gospel and Christian music arena she's worked with, stellar-award-winning producer **Aaron Lindsey** of **New Breed**, stellar and dove award winning artist **Tonex**, and producer **Warryn Campbell**.

Because of her professionalism and talent **Mary Mary** recently supported Dayna by singing background for her at the 2006 Stellar Award kick-off event.

In college she had the opportunity to study under and perform with the incredible legendary **Nancy Wilson** who commented, "this lady has the most interesting sound. It's like no other. She appears to be comfortable doing what she does. She's incredible."

She also had the pleasure of being accompanied by, on many occasions, the late great pianist **Johnny "Hammond" Smith** who continuously encouraged her to pursue her dream.

After completing an R&B demo the Holy Spirit continuously tugged at Dayna for several years until she realized that singing for the Lord was her hearts desire.

"I had to sit still for a long time and focus on God and his WORD, and fast for weeks before it was revealed to me that serving God and leading people to Christ was the most important thing in my life," she said.

"We are very excited to be releasing *Everyday* as the first single," said Mr. M, *40 Entertainment, Inc,* executive producer. "It's definitely time for Dayna to give her testimony."

" For years the music industry has been missing real depth and passion as it relates to the art form itself. Dayna encapsulates vocal prowess and unblemished delivery. Her voice pulls you in. I respect and appreciate her awesome gift," **Tonex**.

-30-

PITCH LETTER

ENTER DATE HERE

Osker Lee
4 Queens Magazine
43170 Walton Ave.
Hollywood, CA 90028

Dear Mr. Lee,

40 Entertainment's producer "Nick Vann Clayton" will soon celebrate 10 years in the music industry. In the interest of featuring the platinum-selling artist in an upcoming issue I have enclosed information for your review.

Fresh on the heels of his increasing success of the hit album "It's Your Boy Nick"—his fastest selling project to date—expectations for the August 30th release, "It's Me Again," his sophomore project, is in full height.

As his combined album sales continue to move well beyond the one million mark "It's Me Again" exhibits energetic songs that exude inspiration and feed the soul. His signature beats and awesome production cater to a diverse audience and showcase his love for music.

The 15-song project delivers flavorful ingredients that make for an undeniable recipe of R&B and hip-hop driven tracks with a twist of soul.

I will contact you in a few days to discuss the possibilities.
Thank you for your time.

Sincerely,
Lynn Meadowood

PITCH LETTER

Date
Name
Title
Publication
Address

Dear:

Ashlye Renee, author of *Where Do I Go From Here?* will be in Houston, Texas August 20 to speak at the Houston Executive Women's annual conference. Her keynote is titled, "prioritizing Your Life."

Facilitating more than 600 seminars throughout the U.S. and Canada, Renee is a motivational speaker and author described as dynamic and spellbinding who has been featured on various networks as CNN, NBC, CBS, and radio stations throughout the U.S.

Her own experience deems her an expert on personal success and is displayed in her #1 international-best-selling book where she reveals the secrets of a proven success formula by offering the reader an easy-to-understand blueprint to creating a stress-free life.

I hope you will consider interviewing her while she's in Houston. I will follow up with you in a few days to discuss the possibilities.

Sincerely,

MUSIC CD PRESS RELEASE

Contact:
Pc Public Relations & Management
323-XXX-XXXX
pcpub@earthlink.net

FOR IMMEDIATE RELEASE

ARTEMIS GOSPEL RELEASE
"RiZen 2"
Rizen To The Second Power!

Nashville, TN--Fresh on the heels of the success of their hit self-titled debut album, *RIZEN*, expectations are high for ***RiZeN 2***, their sophomore release on Artemis Gospel (formerly Light Records), set to release on May 17, 2005.

As their combined album sales and notoriety continue to increase, ***Rizen 2***, the group's sophomore album, exhibits energetic and heart-felt songs that feed the soul. While the group's harmonies and precise production cater to a diverse audience and showcase their love for entertaining, the project exudes spirituality and their dedication to their Lord and Savior.

With ***RiZen 2***, the energetic ladies from Saginaw, Michigan deliver 12 songs full of flavorful ingredients that make for an undeniable recipe of R&B, gospel and inspirational driven melodies, with a twist of soul. But it's their signature foot stomping, and hand clapping that bring it all
together for one big dish of joyful music.

According to group member Adriann, this new album is more of RiZen and has a lot to do with the girls' personal experiences.

-more-

Sanchez Harley, the group's principle producer stated, "there are a lot of diverse influences you can hear in what they do. Rock, R&B, pop ballads are all part of the mix, with a very high energy level throughout, and it uniquely positions them to reach audiences that are both older and younger, traditional and contemporary".

"Over There," the hand clapping foot stomping hit written by Aundrea and Adriann along with their brother Ayron, is reminiscent to "View Of The City" from their debut project. The group's collaboration on "Hold On" demonstrates their continued creative growth. From the sensational, superb production of "Clap Your Hands" featuring the infamous percussionist Sheila E., and the R&B groove of "Praise Him Just A Little While," to the powerful four words of "Jesus You're My Light" to straight up churchin' with "Over There" their signature foot stomping, hand clapping and harmony bring it all together for one big dish of joyful music.

Although the group is still fairly new to the music industry when measured by years, their sudden rise to the top has empowered them to continue to break new ground. Their career has been filled with accolades including a Stellar Award, Dove Award nominations, and a slot on the

"Sister's In The Spirit" tour with Juanita Bynum, Yolanda Adams, Sheila E., Kelly Price and Martha Munizzi. They also were co-hosts for the pre-tape Dove Awards telecast, toured with Byron Cage, and we must not forget the outstanding performance on TBN that catapulted their career.
Through its entirety the overall project proves that RIZEN is the definitive next generation Gospel artist.

#

TV APPEARANCE PRESS RELEASE

FOR IMMEDIATE RELEASE

GOSPEL MUSIC DARLINGS "RIZEN" REUNITE WITH PROPHETESS JUANITA BYNUM ON TBN!

Nashville, TN--As they continue to promote their sophomore release, *RiZen 2,* Artemis Gospel (formerly Light Records) recording artist "RIZEN" will once again be guests of Prophetess Juanita Bynum on TBN TUESDAY, JUNE 21 at 10:00 p.m. EST & 2:00 a.m. EST, and again on WEDNESDAY, JUNE 22 at 5:00 p.m. EST.

RiZen 2, which landed the #6 position on Billboard's Top Selling Gospel Chart, exhibits energetic and heart-felt songs that feed the soul. While the group's harmonies and precise production cater to a diverse audience and showcase their love for entertaining, the project exudes spirituality and their dedication to their Lord and Savior.

The ladies from Saginaw, Michigan deliver 12 songs full of flavorful ingredients that make for an undeniable recipe of R&B, gospel and inspirational driven melodies, with a twist of soul. But it's their signature foot stomping, and hand clapping that bring it all together for one big dish of joyful music.

Sanchez Harley, the group's principle producer stated, "there are a lot of diverse influences you can hear in what they do. Rock, R&B, pop ballads are all part of the mix, with a very high energy level throughout, and it uniquely positions them to

-more-

reach audiences that are both older and younger, traditional and contemporary."

"Over There," the hand clapping foot stomping hit written by Aundrea and Adriann along with their brother Ayron, is reminiscent to "View Of The City" from their debut project. The group's collaboration on "Hold On" demonstrates their continued creative growth. From the sensational, superb production of "Clap Your Hands" featuring the infamous percussionist Sheila E., and the R&B groove of "Praise Him Just A Little While," to the powerful four words of "Jesus You're My Light" to straight up churchin' with "Over There" their signature foot stomping, hand clapping and harmony bring it all together for one big dish of joyful music.

Through its entirety the overall project proves that RiZen is a permanent fixture in the gospel music industry.

-30-

MUSIC CD PRESS RELEASE

FOR IMMEDIATE RELEASE

BESTSELLING AUTHOR AND PASTOR DAVID G. EVANS ADDS MUSIC CD TO HIS INAUGURAL BOOK "HEALED WITHOUT SCARS"
The Healing Process Continues

Evans' first album on premiere label Abundant Harvest Entertainment, Inc, set for mainstream retail release February 1, 2006

VOORHEES, NJ-----Abundant Harvest Entertainment, Inc, is proud to announce the debut retail release of Bishop David G. Evans' new release, "Healed Without Scars," the musical expression of the bestselling book "Healed Without Scars," on February 1, 2006.

The 14-track project, produced by the very eclectic Pastor Lonnie Hunter (Excellence and Stellar award nominee), is described as an "uncommon musical experience" with exceptional production, and introduces an exciting variety of styles from talented vocalists. It speaks of everyday issues and is filled with R&B tunes and heartfelt ballads while maintaining the integrity of the spiritual message.

A cohesive work of art that leads you to a place where you feel open and free to let go and give your problems to God, begins with an inspiring intro, "I'll Let Nothing Separate Me," that simply reminds us to never let anything separate us from God.

The lead track, "Cause Of My Pain," coupled with a concept-video, is a hypnotic R&B tune with smooth vocals bound for mainstream radio.

-more-

"Life" is an R&B tune that describes the backstabbing, lies and all the drama that comes with life.

The sweet sound of Tia Pittman on "Created To Be Whole" is reminiscent of R. Kelly's "I Believe I Can Fly," while "To Praise Him" ministers to you in a jazzy, laid back vibe.

"My Child," "I Will Trust," "The Harvest" and "Let It Be Me" are heart-felt ballads that minister to the soul, while "Ready To Say Yes" pumps it up and takes you to church!

Bishop Evans does an amazing job of narrating over a sweet vocal background arrangement on "Reach Out To Jesus."

Other notable songs include "According To Your Faith," and Remove The Mask."

The last song on the album, the title track "Healed Without Scars," will break you down and have you flat on your face begging for God's help. This song completes the project and will minister to anyone who has been hurt by abuse, disappointment, fear, rejection, abandonment, etc. This is the anthem for the hurt.

"I am continually amazed at the strategic, sovereign plan of God," said Evans. "He brings people together from varied life experiences and contexts. This CD is the culmination of the varied experiences and inspirations of its participants."

Central South, and Anchor will distribute the album in the Christian marketplace.

For more information, go to www.davidgevans.com.

# # #

COMMUNITY -PRESS RELEASE

FOR IMMEDIATE RELEASE

Deron Cloud Gives Back To The Atlanta Community

An Effort To Educate, Motivate, And Mobilize The Atlanta Community In The Fight Against HIV/AIDS, STD's And Teenage Pregnancy

November 30, 2004--Atlanta, GA--In the interest of breaking the chain Deron Cloud (*The Boyfriend Girlfriend Thang!*) and Bishop Eddie Long join forces to raise awareness of STD's, AIDS, and teenage pregnancy by hosting the production of *The Boyfriend Girlfriend Thang!* at New Birth Missionary Baptist Church Tuesday December 7th @ 6:30p.m located at 6400 Woodrow Road, Lithonia, GA 30038.

According to the CDC, (Center For Disease Control) located in Atlanta, GA, as of 2003 the number of new AIDS cases were 42,745, live births to 15-19 year olds were 425,493, and as of 2001 the number of new syphilis cases were 31,575, new Chlamydia cases 783,242, and new gonorrhea cases 361,705.

In an effort to stop the epidemic, invitations to experience *The Boyfriend Girlfriend Thang!* have been extended to all middle and high schools in the Atlanta metropolitan area. The school having the most attendance will receive $3,000 from Bishop Eddie Long and will be matched by Soldiers Outreach to total $6,000.

The Boyfriend Girlfriend Thang! a one-man-stage play produced, directed and starring Deron Cloud, pastor of The Soul Factory and founder of Soldiers Outreach,

-more-

has propelled itself into a sought after production throughout the U.S., and in a matter of six weeks this dynamic production has reached over 35,000 people in the metropolitan Atlanta area alone.

Featuring the hottest music and entertaining stage performance, Cloud goes all out to expose the schemes that women fall for causing them to make bad relationship choices. It also reveals ways to avoid being the next victim of heartbreak, teenage pregnancy and the like by promoting abstinence.

Drawing crowds of thousands to major venues, it is one of several productions produced by Cloud that incorporates drama and the arts allowing him to inform and entertain communities that thirsts for a message in a today-generation language.

For more information on Deron Cloud go to www.soldiersoutreach.com

# # #

SEMINAR PRESS RELEASE

Renee M.
Pc Public Relations & Management, Inc.
323-999-9999
rmpcpub@earthlink.net

FOR IMMEDIATE RELEASE

Tasai Salon & Day Spa Sponsor Largest Southern California Schwarzkopf Hair Cutting Seminar

Internationally Acclaimed Hairstylist Billy Yamaguchi Host Feng Shui Concept Show; A Holistic Approach To Beauty.

SAN DIEGO, California--Tasai Salon & Day Spa will sponsor a hair-cutting seminar and Feng- Shui concept show for Schwarzkopf, Inc. Color Company Sunday March 18th from 11:00 a.m. – 3:00 p.m.

The event will be held at Tsai Salon & Day Spa and hosted by Billy Yamaguchi, International spokesperson for Schwarzkopf, Inc. Color Company. The Feng Shui concept show; *A Holistic Approach to Beauty*, will target salon and spa owners, hairstylists, and skincare professionals.

Tasai Salon & Day Spa, a space boasting four spacious, private, multipurpose rooms with more than forty different treatments, Vichy showers, an 18-chair hair salon with a private hair-augmentation room, and a separate salon for men offering skin care, barbering, body care and massages, manicures, pedicures, and a 24-hour access to CNN and ESPN.

-more-

President and co-owner of Yamaguchi Salon and Coastal Day Spa, Yamaguchi at Spa Ojai in Ojai, California, and Yamaguchi at Spa La Quinta in La Quinta, California, Yamaguchi has conducted educational classes throughout the United States and leads seminars and workshops throughout Europe, Asia, South America, Canada, the Philippines, and South Africa on the fundamentals and artistry of the hair industry.

According to Tasai owner Joan Jackson, "This will be the first of many seminars and workshops Tasai Salon & Day Spa will host. We are delighted to host a platform that will educate, inform and unite beauty industry professionals from all areas of the world."

# # #

MILESTONE PRESS RELEASE

Contact: Lisa Lucci
LL@cool.net
555-555-5555

FOR IMMEDIATE RELEASE

FOOTBALL VETERAN JOHN JACKSON REACHES
NFL MILESTONE IN GAME 200

LOS ANGELES, CA--Cincinnati Bengals offensive lineman John Jackson reached the NFL milestone Sunday December 9, 2001 after playing in his 200th game.

Seven times in his fourteen-year career, Jackson started and played in the entire 16-game season. His career began when the Pittsburgh Steelers made him a 10th-round draft pick in 1988 out of Eastern Kentucky.

Jackson, a Cincinnati native, played in the first Bengals season in 2000 after ten years with the Pittsburgh Steelers and two years with the San Diego Chargers. Noted as being a key figure in a mostly young locker room, he declined unrestricted free agent status to sign for two-years with the Bengals.

Jackson's greatness extends not only on the field but also in his personal life. He and his wife Joan started the John and Joan Jackson Foundation (based in Cincinnati), which support Boys & Girls Clubs and Habitat for Humanity. They also appeared on The Oprah Winfrey Show and brought $5,000 worth of coins for Oprah's Angel Network, which sends one child from each U.S state to college. John Jackson has established himself not only as a humanitarian for youth, but as a successful businessman and a legendary athlete who has graced the NFL community.

#

BUSINESS ANNIVERSARY PRESS RELEASE

FOR IMMEDIATE RELEASE   Contact: Ricky Riley
                                        PCPRmedia@moonlink.net
                                        555-555-5555

JO-TES SALON & DAY SPA CELEBRATE ONE YEAR IN BUSINESS

*Neighborhood Businesses and Beauty Representatives
Come Together For A Fun Filled Week*

San Diego, CA –*Jo-tes Salon & Day Spa*, in conjunction with neighborhood businesses, will celebrate their one-year anniversary Saturday October 6 at their facility located at 10549 Scripps Poway Parkway, Suite D, San Diego, Ca. from 10 a.m. – 2 p.m.

Jo-tes Salon & Day Spa will celebrate their one-year anniversary by offering a 50% price cut to their customers. For five days customers will also sample an array of some of the best beauty products on the market and network with representatives from Bath Bloomers, Affirm, Schwartzkopf, Phytomer, Color Lab, Dermalogica and Bumble & Bumble.

Jo-tes Salon & Day Spa, owned by Joan Jackson and husband John Jackson of the Cincinnati Bengals is a 3400-square-foot establishment offering services to men and women including an array of therapeutic and beautifying services and products. From "Joan's Favorite to the "John Jackson Sports Facial," the spa provides a luxurious retreat for the mind, body and soul.

The event is partially sponsored by Brueggers Bagels, Scripps Poway Eye Care and other organizations.

# # #

PRODUCT PRESS RELEASE

FOR IMMEDIATE RELEASE

Contact: Cicely Range
CR@pcpub.net
(333) 333-3333

CELEBRITY HAIRSTYLIST/SALON OWNER TRACCI JOHNSON CREATES SIGNATURE SHINE HAIR GLASS

Los Angeles, Ca.--March 25, 2003 -- Celebrity hairstylist/salon owner Tracci Johnson creates *Signature Shine Hair Glass* as the first release of her signature collection. It was announced today.

Traci Johnson *created Signature Shine Hair Glass* after continuously trying other "shine in a bottle" products that didn't live up to their slogan. "I tried several products that were either too heavy, didn't shine enough, or did not revitalize the hair after use," she said.

A dime size amount of *Signature Shine Hair Glass* rubbed on the hair will revitalize, stimulate, restore and rejuvenate hairstyles after one week from the salon. Its lightweight ingredients prevent buildup and lifeless hair and give hair the appearance of a fresh look with maximum shine.

Voted as one of the top 10 African American stylists by Upscale Magazine, Johnson's celebrity clientele include: "Baby Face, ", Jada Pinkett-Smith, Nia Long, Cee Cee Winans, Natalie Cole, Brandy, Cicely Tyson, Lynn Whitfield and *Trinity 5: 7* to name a few.

Johnson's creations have graced the Grammy's, the Academy Awards, Soul Train

-more-

Awards, The NAACP Image Awards, the Stellar Awards and the American Music Awards not to mention coverage on various CD covers, music videos and television talk shows.

In addition to the signature collection, Johnson is a highly sought-after educator who travels extensively teaching haircutting techniques at sold out seminars.

She has also produced and released an informative instructional video highlighting hair cutting and other techniques entitled <u>Celebrity Finishing: A Tracci Johnson Experience</u>.

Johnson's latest venture is a member of the consulting team for the new ABC network show, "Extreme Makeovers."

When asked to explain her success Johnson replied, "the key to my success is having faith in Christ and surrounding myself with people who lift me spiritually and mentally.

# # #

DONATION PRESS RELEASE

FOR IMMEDIATE RELEASE

Contact: Lisa Lucy
323-333-3333
PCPR@moonlink.net

SKIN THERAPIST TO THE STARS GIVE BACK
Free Five-Star Treatment To Rehabilitated Women

BEVERLY HILLS, California--In the midst of the highly visited historical Old Towne Pasadena, Delord Skincare, owned by Skin Therapist and Educator Traci Williams, will offer free facials to former homeless women on Christmas eve from 10:00 a.m. to 2:00 p.m. at 107 S. Fair Oaks Ave.

Delord Skincare is a private facility offering corrective treatment for people with intensive corrective skincare needs and an array of rejuvenating treatments that cater to its versatile clientele, including celebrities as well as the individual who just wants to be pampered.

"This is my way of giving back and putting smiles on a few faces for Christmas," said Williams.

Specializing in treating individuals who suffer from acne, Williams is a licensed esthetician created the Alternative Acne Therapy treatments in 1990. The alternative is a safe and more effective method to clearing and controlling acne without using internal medication such as the controversial drug acutane or antibiotics. The treatment is taught nationally to estheticians, doctors and nurses nationwide.

-more-

Delord Skincare also offers the Micro-dermabrasion treatment that exfoliates the skin removing fine lines and wrinkles leaving your skin looking vibrant and more youthful and giving the skin a healthy glow. Taught to the general public, Delord Skincare offers weekly anti-aging seminars that teach individuals to combat signs of aging without undergoing "the knife" Traci Williams helped launch The Beauty Learning Center at UCLA Harbor Medical Center and has appeared on The Oprah Winfrey show, BET's Heart and Soul and UPN News. She has been quoted in various beauty and entertainment publications, been a spokesperson for acne at various skincare trade events throughout the United States, and has practiced with some of the most innovative physicians in the skincare industry.

For information on services log onto www.delordskincare.com or call 310-860-SKIN.

# # #

MUSIC CHART DEBUT PRESS RELEASE

11-TIME GRAMMY WINNER SHIRLEY CAESAR DEBUTS #3 ON BILLBOARD GOSPEL CHARTS

I Know The Truth Is The Highest Debut In 22 Years Of Caesar's Career!

NASHVILLE, TN – September 14, 2005--Multiple Grammy-winning gospel legend Shirley Caesar debuts at #3 with new album, "I Know The Truth," on the Billboard gospel charts.

Released on September 6, 2005 ___I Know The Truth___ has achieved the highest chart position, on the Billboard gospel charts, in twenty two years of Caesar's career.

"I Know The Truth," the first single, has been the talk of the music industry as it reveals a more versatile side of Caesar where she raps with Stellar/Dove award-winning artist Tonéx. A song that is definitely out of the box for Caesar exhibiting her ability to collaborate with any artist willing to bring it on.

Other standout songs, on the 12-track project, include "Every Day is Like Mother's Day," in memory of Caesar's mother, and "Jail Bird," a country song about a man on death row who commits himself to God.

"Miracles Still Happen" is a song you must listen to whenever you forget how God heals or whenever your Faith is not where it should be. This song will lift your spirits and remind you of how blessed you are.

-more-

The awesome production of "Give Me A Song" is an upbeat tune that makes you want to move your body continuously.

"I've Been Redeemed" and "Come To The Altar" bring Caesar's signature energetic powerhouse vocals with an abundance of love and encouragement.

"The project itself is vintage Shirley Caesar and offers a few things a little different from the norm for her", said project-producer Sanchez Harley.

Indeed a living legend Caesar has earned numerous accolades including 11Grammys, 13 Stellar Awards, 18 Dove Awards, an induction into the Gospel Music Hall of Fame, and recently honored at Oprah Winfrey's Legend's Ball for her contribution to the arts and entertainment.

# # #

FOR IMMEDIATE RELEASE   Contact: Yasmin Pippo
                                                         pcpip@pc.net

40 Entertainment In Conjunction With *Pc Public Relations & Management, Inc.*

Present

Singer/Songwriter

DAYNA CADDELL RELEASES SINGLE "EVERYDAY (HE'S GOOD)"

Produced by Stellar & Dove Award-winning producer Aaron Lindsey

Hit by a drunk driver, temporarily disabled and forced to walk with a cane for three years, Dayna has overcome major triumphs and is finally back on track working diligently to complete an album that has kept many waiting patiently for over three years.

The first single "Everyday He's Good" will be released to radio and the completion of the project will continue. To complete the project Dayna is working with Grammy, Stellar and Dove Award-winning producer Warryn Campbell (Mary Mary, Brandy Luther Vandross), Grammy Award-winning producer "Nisan" (Missy Elliot, The Soul Seekers, Madonna), Stellar and Dove Award-winning producer Aaron Lindsey (Israel & New Breed, Marvin Sapp, Karen Clarke-Sheared, Darwin Hobbs), Grammy-nominated, Stellar and Dove Award-winning artist Tonex, and newcomer producer Nicholas "Vann" Clayton.

WHAT THE INDUSTRY IS SAYING:

"Dayna's voice is warm and unique and I can't wait for the world to hear her." Erica Campbell—Mary Mary.

-more-

"For years the music industry has been missing real depth and passion as it relates to the art form itself. Dayna encapsulates vocal prowess and unblemished delivery. Her voice pulls you in.   I respect and appreciate her awesome gift."--Tonex.

"Dayna Caddell's vocal abilities and power will cause any and everyone to take notice of her anointing that God has placed on her"--Alvin Williams, The Gospel Music Channel

"Dayna has a voice with range, depth and emotion and I look forward to the rest of the world receiving her gifts from God as she puts it down." – Sheilah Belle, The Belle Report/The Gospel Times Newspaper.

"Dayna, a voice that is heavenly and hypnotic-a voice that the world needs to hear...."--B. Jeffrey Grant-Clark, Vice President, Promotions/Artist Relations Zomba Gospel

# # #

BOOK RELEASE

FOR IMMEDIATE RELEASE
Contact: Brenda Williams
323-993-0773
bfpub@earthlink.net

ENTERTAINMENT PUBLICIST TO RELEASE
"DO-IT-YOURSELF PUBLICITY"

Phyllis Caddell-M, CEO of Pc Public Relations & Management, Inc. has created the ultimate publicity blueprint: <u>Do-It-Yourself Publicity: For Those Too Cheap Or Too Broke To Hire A Publicist</u> distributed by *Lithobit Publishing*.

Because Phyllis Caddell-M is in high demand and receive numerous calls regarding publicity, in particular media relations, she decided to place her knowledge in the format of a book to be used as an everyday tool.

"I decided to write this book to help anyone who can't afford to hire a publicist or PR firm or who feels if they just had a blue print to follow they could do it themselves. I made it simple and plain where anyone who reads it will understand and be able to implement a publicity campaign," said Caddell-M.

The very informative book will explain and help you understand the dynamics of creating and implementing a publicity campaign. From structuring a biography and press release to pitching and understanding the media, this book will give you a handle on the frustration, joy and understanding of public relations.

-more-

<u>Do-It-Yourself Publicity</u> is the first book released under *Lithobit Publishing* and will be available nationwide April 2006.

Caddell-M will release a series of how-to books under *Lithobit Publishing*.

A woman of many talents Caddell-M host publicity-workshops, consults, and travels the world speaking on public relations and related topics.

To purchase the book online go to <u>www.phylliscaddell.com</u>

# # #

BOOK RELEASE

FOR IMMEDIATE RELEASE   Contact: Pc Public Relations
                                         & Management, Inc.
                                         xxx-xxx-xxxx
                                         pcpub@earthlink.net

**BAKER & TAYLOR TEAM UP WITH ALVIN WILLIAMS
TO RELEASE "THE BUSINESS OF MUSIC
FOR THE GOSPEL AND CHRISTIAN INDUSTRY"
NOVEMBER 9TH**

2004--Entrepreneur Alvin V. Williams and music industry pioneer Jay King have joined forces to create the ultimate music business blueprint: <u>The Business of Music for the Gospel and Christian Industry</u> distributed by Baker & Taylor.

Because Alvin and Jay are in high demand and receive numerous calls regarding start-up labels or questions on solving everyday music industry problems, they decided to place their knowledge in the format of a book to be used as an everyday tool.

"When we decided to write this book we wanted to make it simple and plain where anyone who reads it will understand and apply the material to their day-to-day music business operations," said King.

The very informative book will explain and help you understand the dynamics of creating a record label, understanding artist royalties, publishing, manufacturing and distribution, product development, contract formatting, and much more.

"For anyone involved in the music industry, this book is a must," said Williams. "I printed advanced copies to send out for feedback and the next thing I know people were calling me to order the book. I knew this book was going to help people but I didn't know the demand was going to be this great."

<u>The Business of Music for the Gospel and Christian Industry</u> is the first book released under *A. Williams Book Publishing* and will be available nationwide November 9, 2004.

The duo will release a series of books under *A. Williams Book Publishing*: The True Business of Management, Artist Development, Understanding Publishing, and a line of Inspirational motivational books.

"Teaming up with Baker & Taylor gave me the distribution I needed in order to reach retail, universities and libraries," said Williams.

A man of many talents Williams is also director of promotion & affinity marketing for the Gospel Music Channel, the first television network of its kind dedicated to all forms of the gospel music genre; co-creator of "Heard Worldwide," the first reality series to focus on the entire procedure of getting artists signed to a label, Senior judge for Gospel Dream Talent Competition (as aired on BET) and CEO of A. Williams Entertainment Group.

To request press material or booking information, please contact Pc Public Relations & Management, Inc. @ 323-993-0773 or pcpub@earthlink.net

To purchase the book online go to www.alvinwilliams.com.

JOB PROMOTION PRESS RELEASE

FOR IMMEDIATE RELEASE   Contact: XYZ, Inc.
                                        (323) 555-5555

ANTHONY BARNES NAMED VICE PRESIDENT OF ZENON COMMUNICATIONS

Zenon Communications Board of Directors elected Anthony Barnes vice president at their October 14 meeting. Mr. Barnes will take over for Missy Ellis who leaves March 1 to become assistant vice president of the Rattler's Information Bureau.

Before Mr. Banes came to Zenon Communications in 1999, he was the director of operations at Pc Marketing, Inc. His tenure at Pc includes positions as assistant to the director of marketing and director of marketing.

Bernard Woodside, President of Zenon Communications, stated, "I don't think there's anyone more qualified for this position than Anthony Barnes. He is a proven leader for the company and the industry as a whole."

-30-

PRODUCT PRESS RELEASE

FOR IMMEDIATE RELEASE   Contact: XYZ Media
                                         (334) 555-5555

SKIN THERAPIST INTRODUCE PRODUCT LINE
TO ATHLETIC WOMEN

Skin therapist Traci Williams introduced her new line of makeup for the athletic woman in Los Angeles yesterday. At a beauty conference in Los Angeles, Williams said, "Less expensive makeup options for athletic women are long overdue. I had a great time creating a line I thought would look great and last on women on the go."

The new line features foundation, mascara, and lipstick under $20.00. "The best thing about them," Williams says, "is they stay on even when you sweat."

Williams line will be available in all DeLord Skincare salons. Ms. Williams will be in the Los Angeles store on Thursday, June 30 and the New York store on Saturday, July 2 to present her line and take interviews.

- 30 -

MEDIA ALERT

For Immediate Release

Deron Cloud Give Thousands Back To The Atlanta Community

In an effort to educate, motivate, and mobilize the Atlanta community in the fight against HIV/AIDS, STD's and Teenage Pregnancy

<u>Tuesday, December 7</u>

WHO: Bishop Eddie Long & Relationship Expert/Motivational Speaker Deron Cloud

WHAT: A free production of Deron Cloud's The Boyfriend Girlfriend Thang! To raise awareness of AIDS, STD's and Teenage Pregnancy

WHERE: New Birth Missionary Baptist Church 6400 Woodrow Road, Lithonia, GA 30038

WHEN: Tuesday, December 7, 6:30pm-9pm

# # #

According to the CDC, (Center For Disease Control) located in Atlanta, GA, as of 2003 the number of new AIDS cases were 42,745, live births to 15-19 year olds were 425,493, and as of 2001 the number of new syphilis cases were 31,575, new Chlamydia cases 783,242, and new gonorrhea cases 361,705.

In an effort to stop the epidemic, invitations to experience *The Boyfriend Girlfriend Thang!* have been extended to all middle and high schools in the Atlanta metropolitan area. The school having the most attendance will receive $3,000 from Bishop Eddie Long and will be matched by Soldiers Outreach to total $6,000.

The Boyfriend Girlfriend Thang! a one-man-stage play produced, directed and starring Deron Cloud, pastor of The Soul Factory and founder of Soldiers Outreach, has propelled itself into a sought after production throughout the U.S., and in a matter of six weeks this dynamic production has reached over 35,000 people in the metropolitan Atlanta area alone.

Drawing crowds of thousands to major venues, it is one of several productions produced by Cloud that incorporates drama and the arts allowing him to inform and entertain communities that thirsts for a message in a today-generation language.

# # #

BOOK RELEASE MEDIA ALERT

PROFESSED HI-TECH HUSTLER/FORMER COMPUTER HACKER
TELLS ALLIN A SIX-MONTH CRIME SPREE
MR. E. COST SEVERAL COMPANIES OVER $24 MILLION

WHO: Computer hacker turned business mogul Mr. E. author of <u>Memoirs of a Hi-Tech Hustler</u>.

WHAT: Book Release Dinner

WHEN: Thursday, July 19, 2001
6:30pm – 9:30pm

WHERE: Lunaria Restaurant
10351 Santa Monica Blvd.
Los Angeles, CA 90025

WHY: Memoirs Of A Hi-Tech Hustler is a new book by former computer hacker Mr. E. who will be on site to educate business owners on how to avoid being hacked.

Featured on *BET Tonight* and in *Black Enterprise* and *Jet Magazines* as an expert in his field, Mr. E. gives us the uncensored version of his story. He tells about his experiences as a hi-tech hustler and how he now helps protect consumers and organization from becoming victims of computer hackers.

The event is in the form of a murder mystery dinner. The question of the night is "Who wants to kill Mr. E.?" We need your help to solve the mystery. This evening will be full of surprises.

You will receive more information soon. In the meantime, please save the evening of July 19th by calling Madison M., Pc Public Relations and Management, Inc., 323- 555-5555 with any questions.

# # #

CONCERT MEDIA ALERT

"PATTI'S PEARLS" BENEFIT CONCERT
An Intimate Evening With Patti LaBelle and Special Guests

WHO: SINGER SENSATION PATTI LABELLE AND CELEBRITY GUESTS LEND TIME AND TALENT FOR A JOINT FUNDRAISING VENTURE

WHAT: WEST ANGELES COMMUNITY DEVELOPMENT CORPORATION AND THE BILL DUKE SCHOLARSHIP FUND

WHEN: TUESDAY JULY 16, 2002.
7:30 PM

WHERE: WEST ANGELES CHURCH CATHEDRAL
3045 SOUTH CRENSHAW BLVD.
LOS ANGELES, CA 90016

WHY: TO RAISE FUNDS FOR THE WEST ANGELES COMMUNITY DEVELOPMENT CORPORATION AND THE BILL DUKE SCHOLARSHIP FUND.

FOR MEDIA INFORMATION CALL 323-555-5555 or PCPR@moonlink.net.

# # #

TV SHOW FACT SHEET

"THIS IS YOUR LIFE"

SHOW SCHEDULE: Thursdays, 8:00 p.m. (PT)

ORIGINATION: Hollywood, CA

PREMIERE TELECAST: September 20, 2003

CONCEPT: A weekly half-hour reality show that examines high profile celebrities to reveal their lifestyles, hobbies and interests.

PRODUCED BY: Pc Entertainment

CONTACT: Pc Entertainment
Kelly Burnski, 323/555-0773
OR Pc2media.media

SHOW DESCRIPTION:

THIS IS YOUR LIFE explores the lifestyles of various celebrities. Viewers will discover eclectic styles, collections and hobbies as Pc Entertainment takes you inside celebrity homes.

# # #

RECORDING ARTIST FACT SHEET

SHIRLEY CAESAR

† Caesar recorded her 41st CD "I Know The Truth," the first to be released on her new record label Shu-Bel Records-distributed through Artemis Gospel (formerly known as Light Records).

† Caesar has earned numerous accolades including 11Grammys, 13 Stellar Awards, 18 Dove Awards, an induction into the Gospel Music Hall of Fame, and honored at Oprah Winfrey's Legend's Ball for her contributions to the arts and entertainment.

† Caesar has made several notable appearances including a series of commercials for MCI Communications, the televised Live from Disney World Night of Joy, the Gospel According to VH-1, a White House performance for George Bush, and a speech on the Evolution of Gospel Music to the US Treasury Department.

† Caesar performed with Alicia Keys on the BET S.O.S. (Saving Ourselves): The BET Relief Telethon

† Caesar completed her third sold-out run on Broadway, starring in "Born To Sing," the third installment of the "Mama I Want to Sing" trilogy. She played New York's Madison Square Garden in the hit gospel musical, "This Is My Song," with Cissy Houston and Tramaine Hawkins. She has also been involved with four major motion picture soundtracks: Whitney Houston's "The Preacher's Wife," the John Singleton film "Rosewood," and acting roles with Warner Brothers Films' "Love," and Paramount Pictures "The Fighting Temptations" with Cuba Gooding, Jr. and Beyonce' Knowles.

BUSINESS ANNIVERSARY LETTER

Company Name or Letterhead
Address
City, State Zip

Date

Addressee
Address
City, State Zip

Dear:

Thanks to you, we're 10 years old and still going strong! I remember working out of my bedroom before opening up my firm. Now, my business has grown into a successful firm with 15 employees, including account executives, graphic designers, managers, and publicists.

Pc2 Media wants to show you its appreciation. You are invited to join in our anniversary celebration on Saturday, December 9. There will be live music, food and fun. I look forward to seeing you there.

Sincerely,

COMPANY ANNIVERSARY LETTER

Company Name or Letterhead
Address
City, State Zip

Date

Addressee
Address
City, State Zip

Dear:

Two 2 Tango Works, Inc. is celebrating its first year in business. We opened our doors to the public a year ago on January 2. Faith in our clients has helped us grow into a strong firm with accounts throughout the community as well as around the state. We appreciate your taking a chance on us.

In honor of our first anniversary, we are offering all of our regular customers 10 percent off their next service. We want to demonstrate our sincere appreciation for the people who have helped us to grow. Please call us if we can be of service.

Sincerely,

FAVORABLE MEDIA COVERAGE LETTER

Company Name or Letterhead
Address
City, State Zip

Date

Addressee
Address
City, State Zip

Dear Ms. St. Claire:

40 Entertainment would like to thank you and the XYZ News Team for your coverage of our business practices on your special of "striving businesses."

We were pleased to be featured as a business with integrity. Honesty has been a cornerstone of our business dealings since we launched our record label.

Thank you again for your time and your coverage.

Sincerely,

RESPONSE TO CRISIS LETTER

Date

Addressee
Address
City, State Zip

Dear:

I've been at Linden's for three months now. Since my arrival, I've been impressed by the consistent commitment to service from the people here. We're producing a first-rate product and running our company at 100%. Those of you who frequent our store know first-hand what I'm talking about.

In recent days you have undoubtedly read or heard news accounts about the indictment of our president on charges of embezzlement. I want to address this in detail because this is a serious issue, and because you deserve an explanation.

At the outset I want to make one point clear—the allegations concern events that occurred almost three years ago and this investigation has nothing to do with our operations today.

In every respect, Linden's is running an efficient, and professional business and has a long positive history in the community.

I want to sincerely thank you for your support, past and present. We have enjoyed serving you in the past, and we hope we can count on your continued support in the coming months.

Sincerely,

SEASONAL LETTER

Date

Addressee
Address
City, State Zip

Dear Mr. Riley:

February is the month for love. As a valued customer Dot's Flowers will deliver your flowers, plants, balloons or candy anywhere in Savannah and the surrounding areas.

Because Valentine's Day is the busiest day of the year, the demand for deliveries is great. If you choose to have your flowers delivered on February 13, you can receive a 20 percent discount off your purchase. This way, you can be certain that YOU are the first to send your love.

I hope your Valentine's Day is a special one. To place an order for Valentine's Day or any occasion, call (800) 555-ROSE.

Sincerely,

CASE PROBLEMS

To get you more familiar with PR and publicity plans practice these case problems to test your integrity and knowledge, and sharpen your skills.

Case Problem 1

One of your clients is a major city figure who will announce a major city development plan. The morning paper will do a front-page feature if you meet the deadline in two hours. The editor of the paper needs a press release and a photo of your client immediately. The press release is no problem but the only photo you have is of your client 10 years younger with brown hair. His hair and beard is now salt and pepper, so you alter the photo appropriately.

With no delay you submit the photo to the paper without discussing this change with your client. Is this an ethical or unethical public relations move and why?

Case Problem 2

Two 2 Tango Inc., is an upscale design firm that caters to celebrities and professionals. They hire you to stage their 10-year anniversary in Pasadena, California. The owners are requesting a well-known band, the finest food and drinks, celebrities, and major media coverage. You have six months to plan the event. What is your plan of action?

How would you get the media to attend? Who is your target audience? Why would the media attend? Is this company tied to the Pasadena community? How would you develop the menu? Is the event close to a Holiday? What is your angle to get the guests to commit?

Case Problem 3

A record label has hired you to generate publicity for their Grammy award-winning artist who is releasing their sophomore CD and will tour one month after the release. Your purpose is to make sure that the tour receives extensive coverage in the mass media. This will lead to increased sales. How would you structure your publicity plan? What is your goal? What are your objectives? What strategies will you use? How far in advance will you pitch the media? How will you measure your results?

Case Problem 4

You have a skincare salon that specializes in acne and razor bumps. You are located in Hollywood, California and have been in business for five years. Your clients range from attorneys and doctors to a few recording artists. You are ready to launch your product line and want it to be major. Your short-term objective is to generate awareness and double your clientele. Your long-term objective is to have retailers carry your product. What is your plan? How do you get the media to cover your event? What mediums do you target and why? How do you get specific retailers to come out? What strategies will you use? How will you measure your results? Do you need to send a press kit to the media or will a press release and media alert suffice?

Case Problem 5

A pastor from Chicago is taking over a mega church in New York. The business deal will include an in-house TV station, a built-in congregation of 3,000 members and the facility will also be used as a venue for Christian-based concerts, conferences and the like. Create a publicity plan that will ensure awareness. Who is your target audience and what written tactics will you use to inform them? What are your objectives? Can you tie in any special days to turn this into an event? Will you use local, regional or national media? Will it be specialized or trade publications?

"DO-IT-YOURSELF" POP QUIZ

1. The press kit usually contains what four items?

2. The fact sheet is essentially a quick reference tool for whom?

3. The primary written method of conveying news to the media is what?

4. An effective publicity plan or public relations campaign starts with?

5. What are the three most popular special events?

6. What are two electronic mediums?

7. What are two print mediums?

8. What is an EPK?

9. What are the five W's used when writing a press release?

10. If a man jumps 100 feet to his death what type of story is this?

11. If the circus is coming to town and will be giving away fifty tickets what type of story is this?

12. What is the typical media relations process?

13. When writing a press release what should the first sentence state?

14. What is the pitch letter used for?

15. What is the media alert used as and when is it sent to the media?

16. When planning a press conference what should the media receive when entering the venue?

17. When planning a press conference besides the media who should you invite and why?

18. When is it wise to plan a press conference?

19. How does publicity differ from advertising?

20. Before sending information to the media it must be worthy of what?

POP QUIZ ANSWERS

1. Photo, bio, press release and fact sheet

2. Producers, talent bookers and editors

3. Press release

4. Research

5. Grand opening, book signing, CD release party, product launch

6. Radio and TV

7. Newspapers, magazines

8. Electronic press kit

9. Who, what, when, where and why

10. News

11. Feature

12. R.O.P.E process

13. It should four to five of the W's

14. To sell your event, product or service to any particular medium

15. A reminder and should be sent one to two days before and sometimes the morning of the event

16. Press kit or background information

17. Target public officials or anyone related to the field of the event/industry

18. When what you have to say cannot be relayed in writing or by phone

19. Publicity is free and not promised. Advertising is paid for and placed

20. News

FREQUENTLY ASKED QUESTIONS

Q. What do I need to get started as a DIY publicist?

A. A computer, phone, laser printer, email and Internet program, mailing labels, letterhead, press kit folders.

Q. What is the first thing I need to do to let people know I have something to offer?

A. A good way to let it be known that you have a project is to send a press release to the target media and consumers announcing your project.

Q. I plan to release my CD in January when should I begin a publicity campaign?

A. It is wise to start six months in advance. If not, you may miss several publication deadlines.

Q. How do I know what media outlets to target?

A. Research is the key. There are several media directories that are categorized by types of publications, TV programs and the like. Investing in a media directory will save you a lot of time.

Q. If I implement a publicity campaign for my project do I need a marketing plan as well?

A. It is wise to implement a marketing and publicity plan simultaneously. A publicity campaign is not enough. You need other components (promotions, advertising) to get the most for your campaign.

Q. When is the best time to start follow-up calls to media outlets?

A. Usually two weeks after the initial mailing is a good time to start calling back media outlets. This gives your recipient enough time to review your package. Sometimes they need more time so it's best to gauge your calls after the initial call.

Q. When is it a good time to stop contacting a specific editor or producer?

A. If you've made at least six attempts, via email and phone, and still no response I'd say move on and revisit the outlet depending on your deadline. Sometimes the recipient is interested but just can't get back to you in a timely manner. Revisiting sometimes gives them another opportunity to respond.

Q. What is an exclusive story?

A. An exclusive is what you promise to a particular media outlet. Meaning you won't give yiur story to anyone else to print.

Q. How important is it to have an appealing press kit?

A. Very important if you have no relationship with your recipient, or if your company is new. A well-designed and organized press kit gives you some leverage.

Q. If I'm not the best writer should I attempt to write my bio and press releases?

A. Absolutely not. It is imperative that you represent yourself professionally. If you are not the best writer hire a freelance writer to get the job done.

Q. What tools do I need to pitch TV?

A. If you are a performing artist it is wise to have video/DVD footage of your performance. If you are an author, your book should be available electronically and on hard cover. An EPK of you or your client speaking is great to have as well.

Q. How do I retrieve clippings of my project?

A. A clipping service is the best way to go but can cost more than you may want to spend. The less expensive route is to purchase the issue or subscribe to most of the publications you'll be pitching.

Q. How important is it to have a publicity plan?

A. A publicity plan is like a business plan. This is your blue print to a successful campaign. Without it it's easy to lose focus.

Q. How important is it to implement a publicity plan for a project or product?

A. It's extremely important to implement PR in anything you're trying to get to the public or sell. Getting your product placed in magazines or being on a TV talk show is priceless and can definitely increase awareness and sales.

MEDIA DIRECTORIES

Bacon's Media Directories – www.bacons.com/directories/maindirectories.asp

Bacon's Media List Online – www.medialistsonine.com

Broadcasting & Cable Yearbook – www.bowker.com

Burrelle's Media Directory – www.burrelle's.com/indexmd.html

Media Finder – www.mediafinder.com

Media Map Online - www.mediamaponline.com

National Directory of Magazines – www.mediafinder.com/secure/product1.cfm

Online Public Relations – www.onine-pr.com

Radio Publicity – www.radiopublicity.com/gp

NEWSLETTERS

Media Map – www.mediamap.com/webpr

InternetPRGuide – www.internetprguide.com

Ragan Communications – www.ragan.com

The Tip Sheet – www.plannedtvarts.com

Radio-TV Interview Report – www.freepublicity.com

The Publicity Hound – www.publicityhound.com

PUBLIC RELATIONS ORGANIZATIONS

International Association of Business Communications
www.iabc.com

Public Relations Society of America
www.prsa.org

Public Relations Student Society of America
www.prssa.org

Publishers Publicity Association
nlatimer@randomhouse.com

GLOSSARY

Account Executive- A person in a public relations firm who is in charge of and works on a client's file.

Advisory – An announcement or notice that serves to advise the media of the holding of a press conference.

Angle – The hook. It relates to the point of view from which a release or news story is written, to interest a particular audience.

Bio – A briefing for the purpose of providing background information, usually one to two pages, on a client or company.

Clip book – a collection of newspaper clippings about a client collected by the publicist. Usually kept in a binder.

Editor – Director of a newspaper's or news and editorial department.

> **Associate Editor** – Director of the editorial and commentary pages.
> **Managing Editor** – Manager of news operations, to whom the city editor and other news editors answer; the person to whom most press releases are addressed.
> **City Editor** – Director of the local news staff.

EPK (electronic press kit) – A video used to capture the individual or company using background information, photos, company accomplishments and usually an interview with the CEO or spokesperson. This also helps the producer of a television show decide whether or not they want to book the company representative.

Exclusive – A piece of news sent to a medium with the privilege of using it first.

Fact Sheet – a listing of details about a client or event usually inserted in a press kit.

Feedback – Reaction from those affected by an activity or public relations material about a situation.

Focus Group – Panel of people or representatives of the audience a publicist desires to reach, who are asked to give their opinions of proposed programs.

Gatekeeper – Editor, reporter, news director, or other person who decides what material is printed, broadcast, or otherwise offered to the public.

Hype – The promotion of celebrities, books, companies, and the like, through shrewd use of the media.

Image building – Protection and enhancement of the reputation and look of an organization or individual.

Internship – Temporary employment, by a student or a professional, to obtain work experience.

Libel – Mainly defamation by written or printed words but also, as interpreted by the courts, by broadcast.

Media database – a computerized directory of individuals and departments within the media to whom publicity pitches are made.

Media relations – the vital function of public relations dealing with the preparation of news and information for use in the press and other media.

Pitch – an oral or written solicitation by a PR person on behalf of a story or event.

Placement – the acceptance and appearance of a news item, feature story, or other release in a magazine, newspaper, or broadcast medium.

Positioning – The practice of creating corporate identity programs that establish a place in the market for a company and its product. The effort to get ahead by doing something first.

Press conference – Meeting at which the spokesperson for an organization delivers information to reporters and answers their question; *sometimes called a news conference.*

Press kit – Folder containing news/press releases, photographs, bios, and fact sheets sent   to the media to introduce or support a pitch.

Spokesperson – a person designated to speak for another or for a group.

Trademark – Name, symbol, or other device identifying a product, officially registered and legally restricted to the use of the owner or manufacturer.

Video news release (VNR) – A news release transmitted to TV stations via satellite or videotape.

THE AUTHOR'S JOURNEY

While in college I interned (for free) at various entertainment-PR firms. Interning is very important if you want to get the real deal on how PR firms operate, determine what direction you want to go and to witness the chaos in living color. Did I say chaos? I meant situations, disagreements, tantrums, et cetera. Anyway, the most memorable internship had to be when I worked for free, yes free, at a top entertainment PR firm located in Hollywood, California. Although this was not my favorite internship it was my most memorable. I worked three days a week, I had no assigned desk, and parked on the street three to four blocks away because the owner was too cheap to pay for parking. I witnessed the company owner's battle it out on a weekly basis and had the chance to see that it's not all fine and dandy in the entertainment world, specifically the entertainment PR world. Lights, camera, drama!

My favorite internship was at a major entertainment company where I was the publicity coordinator. Fancy title huh? Yeah right. It was a nice title that really meant publicity gopher. But hey I was a paid gopher and the pay wasn't so bad. My duties included bending, climbing, running and sweating. In plain English I was responsible for keeping photography slides together, faxing press releases, mailing press kits, assembling press kits, and keeping the product room in order.   I knew if I were going to get the training I needed to get ahead this would be the place. You see interning is what you make it and I was going to make this the best stepping stone ever. Whenever I got the chance I would snoop around because my goal was to start a file that I could take with me and use for the future. Samples like press releases, biographies, and media lists would come in handy in the long run. I knew one day I would be in a position where my file would be of service to me so I copied papers, I listened intensely and asked many questions because I knew that the more I knew and experienced would make me a better candidate for the next venture and if I worked really hard and proved myself I could be promoted. Right?

Even though this was my favorite internship there were a few glitches that I need to mention. It wasn't the co-workers who made this my favorite place but the environment, the hustle and bustle and executives climbing the corporate ladder, inspired me. The publicity department, where I worked, consisted of four people all women. There was the vice president of publicity whose biggest fear in life was being alone, poor, and on the streets. Her assistant who was my link to reality was the only stable person in the department besides me of course. There was also the publicist who specialized in events that couldn't spell a lick, threw tantrums, and longed for a relationship with a guy who couldn't care less about her who thought I was her little spell checker.

Then there was the senior publicist who specialized in media relations. Let's see how should I describe her? She was a hypochondriac who claimed every illness and praised her homeopathic guru as if he were God. Don't get me wrong I have a few favorites in the natural healing industry but come on! And then there was me, the publicity gopher who could run circles around at least two of the four. Well at least I thought so in my mind.

So you see I knew that if I was going to move up in that department I'd have to wait for the lovesick psycho to get carried away in a straight jacket or the hypochondriac to believe her own hype and finally ball up in a bubble in fear of catching a germ. With that in mind I decided to gather as much information as possible and prepare to move on.

After one year of the soap opera and after my internship had come to an end, I left on a good note and never looked back. I had no desire to try to stay on or apply for another position at the company. I needed a fresh start, a new outlook and definitely a change of scenery. I felt good about my decision but at the same time I was scared because I would soon be a statistic. Unemployed!

I gave myself two weeks to figure out my game plan. Even though I learned a lot from being a publicity coordinator at a major entertainment company, I wanted to be in the music industry. This is what I yearned. Music is my roots. After two weeks to reflect on the mini soap opera I decided that signing up with a temp agency would be a great way for me to experience aspects of the entertainment industry and make a sound decision as to what I liked and what area I could best apply my skills.

If I was to experience the vast duties of the PR world and it's politics, I would need more hands-on experience. My choice was to temp at various PR firms and entertainment companies.

My two weeks were up and early Monday morning I was up with the sun. I was excited because I was signing up with one of the top entertainment temp agencies in Hollywood, CA. So I put on my favorite navy suit. Who am I kidding? My only navy suit and I was on my way to new experiences and greater heights. I felt good, I looked good and most importantly I smelled good.

I heard about the agency through a friend and was warned to stay away from a certain representative, let's say her name was "Lucy". She was extremely rude, had an attitude for no reason. Looking back I guess she was not happy with her life but the lady did her job quite well. How do I know? Because the moment I signed with the agency I was working consistently where I rarely had time for myself. The whole idea of temping, I thought, was to have the freedom of working when I wanted to work and experience various companies at my leisure. Not in this case. "Lucy" had me temping at some of the most reputable entertainment and public relations companies in the Los Angeles, Hollywood and Beverly Hills areas. One of the most pleasant places I temped was at Imagine Entertainment. A company owned by Ron Howard. A-list actors and producers were constantly in and out of the company including Tom Hanks and his wife Rita and Meg Ryan. I was offered a publicity position but turned it down for many reasons. One, I had my own agenda. Two, I had my own agenda. And three, I had my own agenda! So I was off to yet another temp job. This particular company was in Hollywood. The more upscale part of Sunset Blvd. I learned a lot from this internship. I saw a lot of cutthroat nonsense, arguing over petty things and down right witnessed someone stealing another's idea and boldly presenting it at a meeting as if it was their own. At this particular job I remember taking my lunch breaks and walking by upscale restaurants and retail stores promising myself that one day I would be eating and shopping at those same stores but as a PR executive.

My last stop as a temp turned into a permanent gig at a major record label. I was only there to answer phones and save money to start my company. But fate didn't have it that way. The owner of the company found out that I had a public relations background and offered me a position in the publicity department and in one month I was working as a publicity assistant. This was a very interesting move. I moved from one area where I saw big name rap artist and producers coming in and out of the office to sharing an office with my new boss. Did I mention that he would lock the door so no one could enter the office? I felt like I was trapped. How could this be a promotion? Well let's see. I would learn to pitch recording artists to media outlets, add important contacts to my media list, meet artists in the music industry and basically learn from one of the most experienced publicist in the industry. I'd say it was a promotion. This was my first full-time job in the music industry as a publicist. I wasn't the head publicist but hey I was assisting one. Again, I'd just have to make the job what I wanted it to be. During my prison term, because that's what it felt like, I experienced and witnessed things that amazed and surprised me but I was there for a reason and a few seasons and after gaining a tremendous amount of experience it was time to go. Not only did I leave with a huge chip on my shoulders but also on my way home I had an epiphany. I realized that this was the opportunity for me to start my company.

I buckled down and began the first step of starting a PR firm. I needed a name. Something catchy but obviously that related to me. I needed an image and was able to barter with one of my sisters to design my letterhead and pick her brain for a company name. In a few weeks she produced my image: logo, business cards, stationery, letterhead and envelopes. Thank God for talented siblings. I shopped for an inexpensive computer and a good but inexpensive fax machine and printer, and subscribed to Billboard and a few other music-industry trades. Why? If I was going to be in the music industry I needed to keep up. I had to be on my toes in case Michael Jackson was looking for a new publicist! Can't a girl dream? But seriously I had to be ready when I landed that big client that would take me to greater heights.

As I began to set up my makeshift office, in my bedroom, I received a call and in a matter of days I found myself, once again, straying from my dream and working in a licensing department for a literature company. This temporary job offer came by surprise but it was a way to finance my new business and it was short term of course. Five months to be exact. Unfortunately the five-month job turned into three months due to lack of funds and I was once again unemployed and trying to start my business. A couple of days before my temp job ended I got a call from a casting agent friend who happened to have an actor friend starring in a major sitcom on the FOX network, who just happened to be looking for a publicist. I met the actor. He was nice, funny and cheap! We talked about what I could do for him and what I had done in the past. I could easily tell him of my prior jobs but it was the "what can you do for me" thing that stumped me. After an in-depth conversation he hired me. I was happy, scared and in shock. I had no idea how to begin his publicity campaign. I had a lot of research to do and had to create a bio, assemble press kits, write pitch letters, meet his manager, etc. I was exhausted just thinking about the work ahead of me. If I could do right by this client I would be on my way. I spent a lot of time researching I created a booklet of magazine articles and pitch letters from my previous jobs and used them as templates until I could come up with my own style of writing. I called my media contacts I made from previous jobs and told them who I was representing. Immediately doors began opening and in a matter of three months I had my client confirmed in national publications. Although he was not impressed at all I was jumping for joy. This was a load off my shoulder and boost of confidence but I realized this man was a star on a sitcom and to him this was no big deal. I knew I had to come up with something huge. So huge it would make his head spin. I stayed calm and put on my thinking cap. I remembered in college my professor said the easiest way to get coverage was to capitalize on holidays (tie-ins). It was mid February and too late to pitch for Valentine's Day but Mother's Day was approaching. I knew it was too late to pitch my client to magazines but that I might be able to catch a talk show producer in the beginning stages of a Mother's Day special. I remembered I had met a publicist (thank you Robin), from networking of course, who worked at the Oprah Winfrey Show. I called her to get the inside scoop and she connected me to one of the show producers. I told her whom I represented and that I was hoping to get him on the special they were preparing for Mother's Day. One thing led to another and voile! I placed my first client, of five months, on the Oprah Winfrey Show! Now, my client was excited. He was so impressed with my work and I could tell because he was finally looking to me for cues instead of trying to tell me how to do my job. Of course he was the actor but in my mind I was the star! I accomplished something that I thought would take years. It was all about timing, relationships, persistence and faith. For a few weeks I was sitting on top of the world. That was the biggest boost of confidence I had ever received. Since that day I never looked back and sixteen years later I still enjoy my career.

Phyllis Caddell-M

Thank You Too!

Some of the writing samples, in this book, are of actual clients I've had the pleasure of representing. If you are interested in booking them or buying their product their contact information is listed below.

Alvin Williams
Author – "The Business of Music for the Christian and Gospel Industry"
www.alvinwilliams.com
alvinwilliamsawe@aol.com

Benaleigh Jewelry
vanclaytonjams@cs.com

Bishop David G. Evans
Author – "Healed Without Scars"
d.evans1@rcn.com
www.abundantharvest.com

Dayna Caddell
Songwriter/urban inspirational singer
www.daynacaddell.com
40 Entertainment
626-795-4077

Deron Cloud – Relationship expert, pastor, director, producer
"The Boyfriend Girlfriend Thang!" and other productions
www.soldiersoutreach.com

Dr. Traci Williams
DeLord Skincare
www.delordskincare.com

"Out Of Eden"
jim@chaffeemanagement.com

Rizen
www.rizen.biz

Shirley Caesar
www.shirleycaesar.com

Two2TangoWorks Design
Two2tangoworks@earthlink.net
626-795-4177

Quick Order Form

Fax orders: 626-795-1443. Send this form.

email orders: pcpub@earthlink.net
web site orders: www.phylliscaddell.com

Please send the following book Do-It-Yourself Publicity: For Those Too Cheap Or Too Broke To Hire A Publicist.

Please send FREE information on:

____ Speaking Engagements ____ Publicity Workshops ____ Consulting

Name:

____

Address:

____

City: _________________________________ State:_______ Zip:_____________

Telephone: _______________________________ Fax: ______________________

email address:____

$19.95 + sales tax: Please add 8.25% for products shipped to California addresses.

Shipping and handling: U.S. $5.00 for first book and $3.00 for each additional book International: $10.00 for first book; $6.00 for each additional product.

Payment: _______Visa ______MasterCard ______ Cashier's Check/Money Order

Card number: ____